Food Allergies

NUTRITION & HEALTH

Food Allergies

KEVIN HILLSTROM

LUCENT BOOKS
A part of Gale, Cengage Learning

GALE
CENGAGE Learning·

Detroit • New York • San Francisco • New Haven, Conn • Waterville, Maine • London

LIBRARY OF CONGRESS CATALOGING-IN-PUBLICATION DATA

Hillstrom, Kevin, 1963-
  Food allergies / by Kevin Hillstrom.
    p. cm. -- (Nutrition and health)
  Includes bibliographical references and index.
  ISBN 978-1-4205-0720-1 (hardcover)
  1. Food allergy. I. Title.
  RC596.H55 2012
  616.97'3--dc23

2012002945

Lucent Books
27500 Drake Rd.
Farmington Hills, MI 48331

ISBN-13: 978-1-4205-0720-1
ISBN-10: 1-4205-0720-6

Printed in the United States of America
1 2 3 4 5 6 7 16 15 14 13 12

TABLE OF CONTENTS

Many people today are often amazed by the amount of nutrition and health information, often contradictory, that can be found in the media. Television, newspapers, and magazines bombard readers with the latest news and recommendations. Television news programs report on recent scientific studies. The healthy living sections of newspapers and magazines offer information and advice. In addition, electronic media such as websites, blogs, and forums post daily nutrition and health news and recommendations.

This constant stream of information can be confusing. The science behind nutrition and health is constantly evolving. Current research often leads to new ideas and insights. Many times, the latest nutrition studies and health recommendations contradict previous studies or traditional health advice. When the media reports these changes without giving context or explanations, consumers become confused. In a survey by the National Health Council, for example, 68 percent of participants agreed that "when reporting medical and health news, the media often contradict themselves, so I don't know what to believe." In addition, the Food Marketing Institute reported that eight out of ten consumers thought it was likely that nutrition and health experts would have a completely different idea about what foods are healthy within five years. With so much contradictory information, people have difficulty deciding how to apply nutrition and health recommendations to their lives. Students find it difficult to find relevant, yet clear and credible information for reports.

Changing recommendations for antioxidant supplements are an example of how confusion can arise. In the 1990s antioxidants such as vitamins C and E and beta-carotene came to the public's attention. Scientists found that people who ate more antioxidant-rich foods had a lower risk of heart disease, cancer, vision loss, and other chronic conditions than those who ate lower amounts. Without waiting for more scientific study, the media and supplement companies quickly spread the word that antioxidants could help fight and prevent disease. They recommended that people take antioxidant supplements and eat fortified foods. When further scientific studies were completed, however, most did not support the initial recommendations. While naturally occurring antioxidants in fruits and vegetables may help prevent a variety of chronic diseases, little scientific evidence proved antioxidant supplements had the same effect. In fact, a study published in the November 2008 *Journal of the American Medical Association* found that supplemental vitamins A and C gave no more heart protection than a placebo. The study's results contradicted the widely publicized recommendation, leading to consumer confusion. This example highlights the importance of context for evaluating nutrition and health news. Understanding a topic's scientific background, interpreting a study's findings, and evaluating news sources are critical skills that help reduce confusion.

Lucent's Nutrition and Health series is designed to help young people sift through the mountain of confusing facts, opinions, and recommendations. Each book contains the most recent up-to-date information, synthesized and written so that students can understand and think critically about nutrition and health issues. Each volume of the series provides a balanced overview of today's hot-button nutrition and health issues while presenting the latest scientific findings and a discussion of issues surrounding the topic. The series provides young people with tools for evaluating conflicting and ever-changing ideas about nutrition and health. Clear narrative peppered with personal anecdotes, fully documented primary and secondary source quotes, informative sidebars, fact boxes, and statistics are all used to help readers understand these topics and how they affect their bodies and their lives. Each volume includes information about changes in trends over time, political controversies, and international perspectives. Full-color photographs and charts enhance all volumes in the series. The Nutrition and Health series is a valuable resource for young people to understand current topics and make informed choices for themselves.

Navigating the World of Food Allergies

Most American men, women, and children sit down at the dinner table or pick up a plate at the restaurant buffet line with only the mildest concerns about the meal they are about to eat. Will the food be tasty, or will it be overcooked or bland? Are there enough options for the dieter or vegetarian? Should they have seconds, or save room for dessert? Will their finicky youngest child find something nutritious to eat? For a small but growing percentage of people, though, the concerns they face at mealtime are much more serious. Will this food cause me to break out in a rash? Will it trigger hours of vomiting and diarrhea? Could it kill me? These scary possibilities enter into the thoughts of people with severe food allergies with every meal.

People with food allergies account for a relatively small percentage of the U.S. population. Scientists and doctors generally agree that about 15 million Americans live with food allergies. This figure includes nearly 6 million children, about 8 percent of all American kids. Nine million adults also have food allergies, about 4 percent of that population. The number of Americans with food allergies is rising quickly, however, and researchers worry that it is emerging as a major public health issue.

The impact of food allergies, in fact, is already being felt in many areas of American society. Millions of families are restructuring their daily lives to keep allergic family members safe from harm. Schools, summer camps, and day-care centers are rewriting their snack and lunch rules to keep peanuts, milk, eggs, and other highly allergenic foods far away from their students and campers. Youngsters and teens are educating themselves about what they should do in the event that a friend with severe food allergies is struck down by a serious allergy attack.

People with severe food allergies have to take precautions to avoid even trace amounts of common foods such as milk, wheat, peanuts, and shellfish that could be deadly to them.

The biggest life adjustments, though, have to be undertaken by the children and adults who actually live with food allergies every day. This task can be enormously challenging, especially if they have life-threatening reactions to certain foods. People with severe food allergies have to take precautions to avoid even trace amounts of peanuts, milk, wheat, shellfish, and other common food items that are deadly to them.

Nonetheless, millions of men, women, and children who have serious food allergies have managed to find other foods that are both nutritious and tasty. They also lead interesting and fulfilling lives. Sandra Beasley is an award-winning poet who has allergies to dairy (including goat's milk), egg, soy, beef, shrimp, pine nuts, cucumbers, cantaloupe, honeydew, mango, macadamia nuts, pistachio nuts, swordfish, and mustard. She's also allergic to mold, dust, grass and tree pollen, dogs, rabbits, cigarette smoke, horses, and wool. Beasley agrees that all of these allergies have made life more complicated for her and her friends and family, but she also has a successful writing career and a vibrant circle of friends. "Those with food allergies aren't victims," she says. "We're people who—for better or for worse—experience the world in a slightly different way."[1]

CHAPTER 1

Explaining Food Allergies

Each day millions of American children march off to kindergarten, elementary school, middle school, and high school. For the great majority of them, lunchtime is nothing more than a welcome break in the middle of the day and a chance to tame their growling stomachs. These students unpack sandwiches and snacks out of their lunch bags or cruise through the cafeteria line without a second thought, laughing and chattering away. For kids like Caleigh, though, lunchtime is a potentially dangerous part of the day. Caleigh was diagnosed with a serious peanut and tree-nut allergy when she was a baby. As a result, Caleigh's elementary school had to adopt a wide range of policies to protect her from accidental exposure to nuts.

Some of Caleigh's friends and classmates probably do not fully understand why all these special rules are in place. A number of their parents may even express exasperation or impatience about these measures. What is the big deal, they might think to themselves, the school is treating peanut-butter sandwiches as if they were bombs.

As incredible as it may seem, though, food allergies can be just as deadly as any bomb for kids like Caleigh. "It is hard to fathom how the joys of childhood—a peanut-butter sandwich, a warm chocolate-chip cookie, a cold glass of milk—can send a tiny body into battle mode," writes journalist Claudia Kalb. "How just one bite can make the throat itch, the lips swell, the stomach clench in agony. How an immune system, exquisitely designed to protect us against bacteria and viruses, can perceive healthful nutrients as enemies."[2]

Understanding Allergic Reactions to Food

Not all allergic reactions to food are life threatening. In many cases, a person afflicted with an allergic reaction to food suffers unpleasant but nondeadly symptoms like a rash, a runny nose, or sneezing. Whether the reaction is mild or severe, though, the same basic problem is at work. The person's immune system is malfunctioning.

The immune system is a wonderfully complex and hardworking part of the human body. It serves as our first line of defense against nasty germs and dangerous diseases. The immune system creates antibodies, which are proteins that destroy bacteria, viruses, and other microorganisms that can make us sick when they enter our bodies. Food allergies occur, though, when a person's immune system misidentifies healthy food proteins as a threat (like a harmful virus) and mobilizes antibodies to wipe out that threat. In the worst of these cases of mistaken identity, the immune system works so furiously to destroy the innocent food proteins that it does severe or fatal damage to the body it is trying to protect. This same misidentification accounts for allergic reactions to penicillin, pollen, dogs, cats, and other materials that surround us. In other words, says KidsHealth.org, "the thing itself isn't harmful, but the way your body reacts to it is."[3]

Scientists and scholars have described this phenomenon in a variety of ways.

FOOD FACT

Authorities believe that food allergies account for about three hundred thousand emergency room visits a year. Allergic reactions to stings from bees, wasps, hornets, fire ants, and other insects, however, account for an even greater number of hospital trips—five hundred thousand annually.

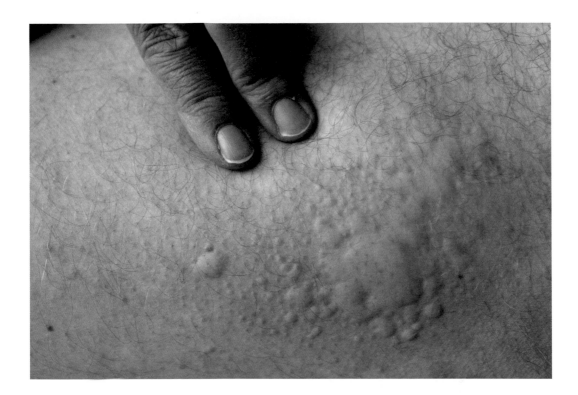

Robert A. Wood is a distinguished pediatric allergist (doctor of children's allergies) at Johns Hopkins University School of Medicine. He compares food allergies to overprotective parents. "Trying too hard to do the best for their children, they often cause more harm,"[4] he claims. Journalist Laura Beil says that a person's immune system is similar to the staff at a busy restaurant. She writes that when peanuts or other common allergenic substances—known as antigens—enter the digestive system after being eaten, they are first greeted by antigen-presenting cells that function like a restaurant hostess. These cells escort guests (the antigens) to their table and alert the waiters. "The waiters," continues Beil,

Not all allergic reactions to foods are life threatening. Often they include nondeadly symptoms such as a rash, persistent runny nose, and/or sneezing.

> are the T cells, which help the body recognize friend from foe. When food allergy develops, the T cells, instead of welcoming the peanut as the valued customer it is, initiate a process that alerts another type of immune cell, called a B cell. B cells make antibodies—the body's bouncers. In the case of food allergies, B cells start to make IgE [immunoglobulin E] antibodies, which when

bound to a peanut protein summon mast cells. Mast cells come armed with chemical weapons. Substances released from mast cells, including histamines and cytokines, lead to the most frightening symptoms of food allergies: hives, vomiting, and anaphylaxis [a severe allergic reaction that afflicts the entire body], which can be deadly. Once the IgE antibodies are on patrol, the peanut protein finds itself on the blacklist, and will be violently ejected by security should it try to return.[5]

The most common symptoms of allergic reactions include itchiness, skin rashes, tingling lips or tongue, runny nose or eyes, difficulty breathing, coughing, sneezing, nausea, and, as shown here, swelling of the tongue.

Food Allergy Symptoms

When mast cells release histamines into the body, a whole bunch of physiological changes take place. Histamine causes blood vessels to widen, which in turn causes allergy symptoms such as sneezing, runny eyes and nose, and hives. Histamine also makes the muscles in the walls of the lungs,

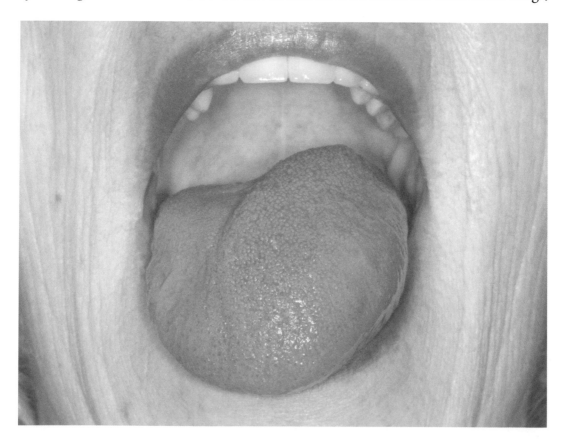

Food Intolerance

People sometimes believe that they have food allergies when in reality they have food intolerances. Food intolerance is a phenomenon in which a person is unable to digest a particular food, or when the food in question irritates the individual's digestive system. In both cases, the problem is with the person's digestive system—not with his or her immune system, as is the case with food allergies.

Confusion about food intolerances and food allergies arises in large part because they can have many of the same symptoms. People suffering from food intolerance may experience stomachaches, diarrhea, and vomiting, which can also crop up with food allergens. Other symptoms of food intolerance include headaches, heartburn, and nervous feelings. One of the key distinctions between food allergies and food intolerance is that food allergies can be triggered by consumption of even a tiny amount of food, whereas food intolerances sometimes do not show themselves unless the person eats the food frequently or in large portions.

The most common food intolerance is intolerance to lactose, a type of sugar found in milk and other dairy products. Some experts believe that as many as one out of ten Americans have some level of lactose intolerance. Other common intolerances include sulfites in red wine and monosodium glutamate (MSG), a popular flavor-enhancing food additive.

stomach, bladder, and other internal organs contract. This contraction can bring on symptoms such as nausea, diarrhea, and difficulty breathing.

The main symptoms of an allergic reaction—whether to food or something else like a bee sting or pollen—include itchiness, skin rashes, tingling lips or tongue, swelling tongue, runny nose or eyes, feelings of tightness in the throat, wheezing or difficulty breathing, coughing, sneezing, nausea, vomiting, and diarrhea.

In addition, doctors say that people who experience severe allergic reactions to food frequently feel a sense of approaching doom at the onset of an allergic attack. As journalist Susan Dominus writes, "People in the early stages of a reaction often feel profoundly that something is very, very wrong, just as they feel the first hints of an itch."[6]

Allergic reactions to food usually crop up within an hour or two of eating, although some may not show up for twelve to twenty-four hours. The more severe reactions, though, often arrive more quickly. Serious reactions frequently trigger symptoms within a minute or two of contact with the allergenic food. Sometimes symptoms even appear within a matter of seconds.

This contact does not always consist of consuming allergenic food, either. People with severe allergies to certain foods can suffer allergy attacks just by touching or breathing in particles of the food. A boy named Eric, for example, is extremely allergic to a wide variety of foods, including milk, wheat, corn, soy, eggs, and peanuts. One time, his mother kissed him goodnight, only to see a lip-shaped welt instantly rise up on his cheek. She immediately realized that her son's skin was reacting to residue from a glass of milk she had polished off a short time earlier. "Merely touching a table surface that had the taint of milk could provoke an itchy rash," says Eric's father. "His eyes watered and itched if he walked by a pizzeria."[7]

The Threat of Anaphylaxis

Minor food allergies frequently involve only one or two symptoms. More serious reactions, though, can wreak major havoc on multiple organ systems, including the skin, respiratory system, digestive system, and cardiovascular system. This type of severe allergic attack is known as anaphylaxis. This potentially life-threatening allergic response frequently develops swiftly, but in some cases the allergic reaction may take an hour or two to reveal itself. One of the worst things that can happen during an anaphylaxis episode is a sudden and extreme drop in blood pressure, which means that the body is no longer pumping enough oxygen-carrying blood to the heart, brain, and other vital organs. This phenomenon is known as anaphylactic shock, and if it starves the brain or other vital organs of needed oxygen for too long, it can result in death.

Anaphylactic shock can unfold in three different ways. In a uniphasic attack, the allergic person experiences a single wave of symptoms. The majority of anaphylactic shock episodes are uniphasic in nature. Another 30 percent or so of attacks are biphasic, which means that the individual suffers a second wave of symptoms after the initial reaction has faded. Finally, anaphylactic shock will occasionally take what is known as a protracted form. In these situations, severe allergic symptoms remain for up to forty-eight hours, even with treatment.

Anaphylactic shock is an extremely scary event for people with allergies and their families. Some people with food allergies who have gone into anaphylactic shock say that even after they recover physically, the memory of the event can be paralyzing. Dean is a young man who nearly died from anaphylactic shock after eating a peanut butter cookie. "I lost 25 pounds right after it happened because I just . . . didn't eat. I was afraid to eat. I suddenly realized there were nuts everywhere." Dean has since regained some of that weight, but he admits that "I'm still nervous all the time. I think about it every time I sit down to eat. I feel a lack of confidence."[8]

An anaphylactic reaction causes a sudden, extreme drop in blood pressure, which means the body is no longer pumping enough oxygen-carrying blood to the heart, brain, and other vital organs.

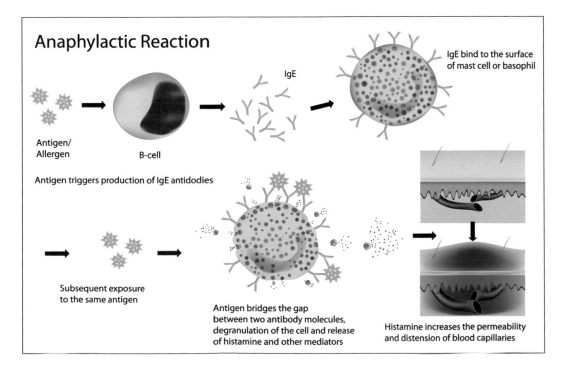

Anaphylactic Reaction

Antigen/Allergen

B-cell

IgE

IgE bind to the surface of mast cell or basophil

Antigen triggers production of IgE antidodies

Subsequent exposure to the same antigen

Antigen bridges the gap between two antibody molecules, degranulation of the cell and release of histamine and other mediators

Histamine increases the permeability and distension of blood capillaries

Anaphylactic episodes usually occur when a person with severe allergies accidentally eats something with the food in it. On rare occasions, anaphylaxis can hit when someone has an allergic reaction to a food that they did not know was deadly. Finally, with peanuts in particular, the lightest exposure to the food can have tragic consequences. In Saguenay, Quebec, for example, a fifteen-year-old girl named Christine who was severely allergic to peanuts went into anaphylactic shock when her boyfriend kissed her. "The boy had eaten peanuts hours before," explains journalist Kevin T. Higgins. "The protein residues in his mouth were sufficient to cause a severe reaction in the peanut-allergic girl. Despite receiving an adrenaline injection almost immediately and being rushed a local hospital, she died a few days later."[9]

Epinephrine Shots

The number one defense that people with severe food allergies have against anaphylactic shock is an epinephrine shot. Epinephrine is a medicine that can relieve the most serious symptoms of allergic reactions—including throat swelling and low blood pressure—and bring attacks under control. Allergists commonly prescribe epinephrine to kids and adults with severe allergies to food or other substances.

Medical device manufacturers have developed a variety of syringe-type devices for injecting epinephrine into the bodies of people with severe allergies. These devices are easy to use—older children can learn to inject themselves—and are similar in appearance to a pen. They deliver medicine immediately into the bloodstream so that it can provide relief right away. Users of epinephrine autoinjectors are typically instructed to make injections into the thigh area when they have to be used. There are many different epinephrine autoinjectors on the market, but the best-known is the EpiPen®. Other popular brands include Twinject®, Adrenaclick®, and Anapen®. Drug makers also make autoinjection doses in two different strengths—a junior version for young children and a full-strength one for older children and adults.

Epinephrine can save the lives of people who experience severe allergic reactions to food, insect bites, and other aller-

A variety of syringe-type devices have been developed by medical researchers for injecting epinephrine, a hormone and neurotransmitter that can relieve the most serious symptoms of allergic reactions.

gens. That is why doctors urge people with severe food allergies to keep their autoinjectors with them *at all times*. In addition, family members, teachers, friends, and parents of friends should all become familiar with autoinjectors and learn how to use them in case the person with allergies experiences an allergic episode. Doctors also say that epinephrine autoinjectors need to be stored at normal room temperatures, away from strong sources of heat or cold.

Many people with severe food allergies say that epinephrine autoinjectors have enabled them to lead much more "normal" lives than would otherwise be possible. As journalist Elizabeth Landau writes about her autoinjector device, "We've had nearly every meal together for the past fourteen years. We've been kayaking on the California coast. We've ridden airplanes, boats, horses, bikes, and an Israeli camel together. . . . The allergy injector has both the dependable and nagging qualities of a protective older sibling. It promises to be there when I need it, but also has to follow me around to make sure I'm OK."[10]

Allergists emphasize, though, that even after the epinephrine has been injected, people with severe allergic reactions still need to call 911 or quickly get to an emergency room. Qualified medical personnel need to make sure that the allergic reaction is under control and does not require further medical intervention.

In addition to carrying epinephrine at all times, people with severe food (or other) allergies should also wear an allergy alert bracelet or necklace at all times. These tags contain information that can help responders provide proper treatment to people who become too ill to explain their condition. Allergy alert products typically include a list of known allergies and the name and telephone number of an emergency contact person. Some of these items also include additional information on personal medical history, health care provider, and additional emergency contact alternatives.

Major Food Allergy Triggers

More than 160 types of food can cause allergic reactions, but 8 types of food account for nearly all food allergies in the United States: eggs, fish, milk, peanuts, shellfish, soy, tree nuts (such as walnuts, almonds, and pistachios), and wheat.

It is relatively easy for people who are allergic to these foods to avoid eating or drinking these items in their simplest form. People with milk allergies abstain from drinking milk; people who are allergic to eggs stay away from scrambled eggs or omelettes at breakfast time; and people who are allergic to tree nuts decline offers of pecan pie. Avoiding these foods completely is tricky, though, because so many of these items are hidden ingredients in *other* food products. People with food allergies (and the parents of children with allergies) thus are forced to act as detectives whenever they go to the supermarket or eat at a restaurant. They have to check food labels closely and ask detailed questions of restaurant staff to make sure that the food they are purchasing is not contaminated with any offending allergens.

Understanding Celiac Disease

Wheat allergies are sometimes confused with celiac disease, which is an ailment of the digestive system. Celiac disease is a condition in which individuals have a negative digestive system reaction to gluten, a group of proteins that are found not only in wheat, but also in other grains such as rye, barley, and oats. This negative response centers on the small intestine, which gradually loses its ability to absorb vitamins and other nutrients. People with celiac disease thus run a higher risk of developing medical conditions like malnutrition, anemia (a shortage of healthy red blood cells), or osteoporosis (loss of bone density).

Most people who have wheat allergies at an early age gradually outgrow the condition. In addition, people with wheat allergies are frequently able to eat other grains without any problems. By contrast, people with celiac disease have to avoid grains of every kind, since they all contain gluten. Celiac disease is also a lifelong medical condition.

Celiac disease is a condition in which individuals have a digestive system that reacts negatively to the protein gluten, found in various grains such as rye, barley, oats, and wheat.

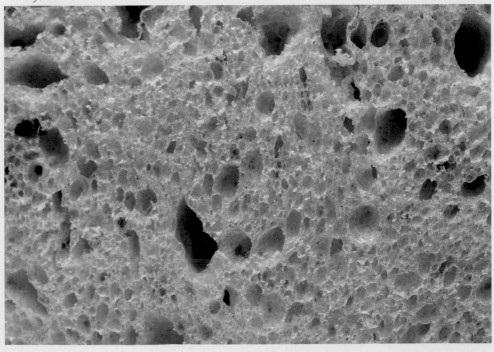

This reality can be pretty depressing, especially for young children and teens with allergies. For example, cow's milk is used to make popular foods like cheese, butter, and ice cream. As Wood notes, however, milk is an ingredient in a "multitude of foods, from baby foods to breads to baked goods and milk chocolate, as well as all kinds of processed foods, so avoiding milk typically involves scratching about half of the most common foods off your grocery list. The good news is that the food industry offers plenty of milk, cheese, butter, ice cream, and yogurt substitutes."[11]

Hidden Dangers in Food

The following is a rundown of some of the foods that frequently contain major allergens. People with food allergies should approach such foods with caution.

Milk can be found in such food products as butter, baking mixes, cheese, chocolate, cottage and ricotta cheese, creamed soups and vegetables, custard, half-and-half, "energy" bars, ice cream, margarine, processed meats, salad dressings, flavored potato chips and tortilla chips, seasoned french fries, sour cream, and yogurt. People with milk allergies also need to be careful when ordering meat from deli counters, because deli meat slicers are sometimes used for both meat and cheese products.

Eggs are traditionally a major ingredient in breads, cakes, cookies, doughnuts, muffins, pancakes, pretzels, waffles, and other baked goods. They also may appear in a wide range of other foods, including beer, candy bars, cappuccino-type beverages, chicken strips and other breaded meats, eggnog, egg noodles, ice cream, icing, marshmallows, mayonnaise, meatballs and meatloaf, pudding, salad dressings, sauces, sherbet, soups, and spaghetti and other types of pasta. Some food items are made with egg substitutes, but allergic buyers should beware, because these foods often just remove the yoke and still contain egg whites.

Peanuts and tree nuts (such as walnuts, almonds, and pistachio nuts) are sometimes present in a wide assortment of baked goods, including breads, cakes, and pastries. They also are commonly found in various breakfast food bars, cereals, chocolate bars and other candies, and ice cream products. Asian foods and vegetarian menus rely heavily on peanuts and other nuts as well. They are used as ingredients in certain salad dressings and condiments, such as barbecue sauce. They are even used as ingredients in some common nonfood products, such as hamster feed, suntan lotion, and shampoo. Peanut and tree nut allergies rank among the most danger-

Four Out of Every One Hundred Children Have a Food Allergy

Percentage of children under age eighteen years who had a reported food or digestive allergy in the past twelve months, by age, sex and ethnicity group: United States, 2007.

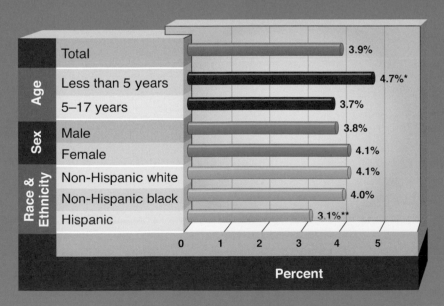

		Percent
	Total	3.9%
Age	Less than 5 years	4.7%*
Age	5–17 years	3.7%
Sex	Male	3.8%
Sex	Female	4.1%
Race & Ethnicity	Non-Hispanic white	4.1%
Race & Ethnicity	Non-Hispanic black	4.0%
Race & Ethnicity	Hispanic	3.1%**

*Significantly different from children aged 5–17 years.
**Significantly different from non-Hispanic white and non-Hispanic black children.

Taken from: CDC/NCHS. National Health Interview Survey. www.cdc.gov/nchs/data/databriefs/db10.htm.

Because peanuts and tree nuts are present in many foods, they contribute to two of the most dangerous food allergies.

ous food allergies, so it is imperative for people who face this issue to proceed carefully—especially in cafeterias and restaurants where strangers are preparing their food.

Fish and shellfish allergens are among the easiest to avoid, because they are not mixed into a lot of other foods. Nonetheless, there are a few food items that should be approached carefully. One is gelatin, which is sometimes made using fish or shellfish bones. Others include bouillabaisse, Caesar dressings, Caesar salads, Worcestershire sauce, and pizzas that are made using anchovies, a small species of fish. It is worth noting that people who are allergic to fish are not always allergic to shellfish such as lobster, crab, and shellfish, and vice versa.

Soybeans and soy products are found in sauces and soups of various kinds, as well as in some baked goods, canned tuna fish, cereals, crackers, and infant formula. Soy is botanically related to green beans, lentils, peanuts, peas, and other legumes, and people who are allergic to one of these foods are often allergic to one or more of the others as well.

Wheat proteins are often hidden in sauces that have multiple ingredients (such as soy sauce) or deep-fried foods that may be cooked with other foods containing wheat. Other ingredients derived from wheat that may spell trouble include bread crumbs, bulgur, cereal extract, club wheat, couscous, durum, einkorn, emmer, farina, flour, hydrolyzed wheat protein, Kamut, matzoh, pasta, seitan, semolina, spelt, sprouted wheat, triticale, and wheat derivates like wheat germ oil and wheat grass.

Soybeans and soy products are found in many foods, such as sauces, soups, baked goods, canned tuna, cereals, and crackers. People who are allergic to soy-containing foods are often allergic to other legumes as well, such as green beans, lentils, and peas.

Outgrowing Food Allergies

Fortunately for children with food allergies and their families, childhood problems with certain foods often fade away with time. According to the Food Allergy and Anaphylaxis Network (FAAN), an estimated 85 percent of children will eventually outgrow their allergies to egg and milk. An even higher percentage of children outgrow allergies to wheat and soy. The food allergies that are most likely to stay with people throughout their lives are the ones to peanuts and tree nuts.

Researchers say that the chances of outgrowing childhood food allergies increase if the child is kept completely away from the allergen in question. "If a five-year-old kid with a potentially fatal allergy to eggs is kept from ever encountering even trace bits of yolk," writes Dominus, "he might grow into a seventeen-year-old with a manageable allergy to eggs, and into a thirty-year-old who can eat like everybody else."[12]

CHAPTER 2

Understanding Rising Rates of Food Allergy

When a young girl named Lydia was diagnosed with severe allergies to peanuts and tree nuts, her mother instantly recognized that her daughter's life would always be more complicated than that of her peers. "Lydia will never be able to go to a birthday party without bringing her own homemade cupcake," she writes.

> Every time she eats in a restaurant, she'll have to bring a card detailing her allergies and pray the chef takes her seriously. I don't want to think about when she's a teenager, too cool to even ask what's in food she's being offered. For now, she can't go over to a friend's house without the friend's mother being fully versed in Lydia's emergency protocol. It's enough work keeping kids entertained and fed; staving off anaphylactic shock may be more than some moms are willing to sign on for.[13]

Researchers say that the number of children like Lydia is on the rise. Allergies to things in the wider environment—especially certain foods—have increased dramatically across the United States over the past half century. Scholars estimate that in 1950 less than 15 percent of the total U.S. population had allergies of one type or another. Today, the American

Academy of Allergy, Asthma, and Immunology (AAAAI) and other research organizations frequently put that number at 50 percent or even more.

Tracking the Jump in Reported Food Allergies

A child undergoes a skin scratch allergy test to identify allergens that cause allergic reactions. Numerous studies indicate childhood allergies are on the rise; thus, there is also a rise in testing for them.

A big factor in this overall increase in allergic reactions is a jump in allergies to food. Not only are more people being diagnosed with food allergies, they also are suffering greater health problems when exposed to those allergens. "Allergists say they're now seeing more children with multiple allergies than ever before, not just to 1950s staples such as milk and wheat—but to global foods we have adopted since, like sesame and kiwi," writes journalist Claudia Kalb. "And allergies many kids outgrow—like those to eggs—seem to be lingering longer than they did in the past."[14]

Food Allergy Among Children in the United States Is Becoming More Common Over Time

Percentage of children under age eighteen years who had a reported food or digestive allergy in the past twelve months, by age group: United States, 1997–2007.

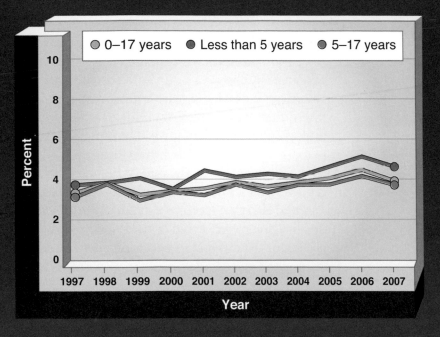

Taken from: CDC/NCHS. National Health Interview Survey. www.cdc.gov/nchs/data/databriefs/db10.htm.

Scientists and doctors can point to a wide range of supporting studies when they declare that food allergies are getting worse. Between 1997 and 2007 the number of children with food allergies rose 18 percent, according to a survey by the National Institutes of Health (NIH). Childhood allergy rates for peanuts alone doubled between 1997 and 2002, according to one study published in the *Journal of Allergy and Clinical Immunology*. The NIH also estimates that about 3 million school-aged children across the United States now have some type of food allergy.

Deaths and hospitalizations from severe reactions to food allergens are on the rise as well. A long-term study conducted by the prestigious Mayo Clinic in Minnesota found that the number of anaphylaxis cases in the United States that were triggered by food allergies increased from twenty-one thousand per year in 1999 to fifty-one thousand per year in 2008.

Allergists admit that it can be difficult to determine exactly how many people have food allergies. In June 2011, for example, *Pediatrics* magazine published a study indicating that fully 8 percent of American kids have at least one food allergy. The study also found that 30.4 percent of children with food allergies had multiple allergies, and that 38.7 percent had a history of severe reactions.[15] Some critics, however, expressed doubts about the reliability of the study, since it gathered data through self-reporting rather than scientific tests conducted by experts.

Food allergy symptoms can closely mirror those that crop up when people get a cold or the flu. Dr. Hugh Sampson, who is chief of the division of pediatric allergy and immunology at Mount Sinai Medical Center, says this is a big problem. "It's always tempting to relate some physical event or symptom back to what you've put in your mouth," according to Sampson. "Hypochondria is a big problem in [tracking food allergies]."[16] In addition, people who have food intolerances sometimes mistakenly believe that their stomach problems are due to food allergies.

Misdiagnosis of food allergies can be a problem. Nonetheless, most experts in the field believe that, according to the most reliable statistics and studies, food allergies now affect about 4 percent of adults and 6 to 8 percent of kids.

There are several leading theories about the root causes of the recent increase in food allergies. Some people believe that it can be attributed to new chemical additives in our food. Others speculate that an increased emphasis on hand washing and other changes in sanitary practices are a factor. Heredity and the timing of children's first introductions to food have also been mentioned as possible factors. Another theory is that food allergies have not increased that much, they are just being diagnosed more often. All of these theories are championed by various allergists, physicians, scientists, and parents of children with food allergies, so they are each worth examining in their own right.

Chemical Changes in Our Food Supply

Some allergy researchers suspect that rising reports of food allergies are due at least in part to rising levels of chemical additives in our food supply. Modern food processing practices involve the use of a lot of different artificial ingredients to preserve food for longer periods of time, change its color and texture, or enhance its flavor. In addition, today's crops are raised with all sorts of chemical fertilizers and pesticides. Meanwhile, dairy farms and livestock operations have become heavily dependent on growth hormones and other chemicals to increase the volume of milk their cows produce or the amount of meat that they can get from individual cows, chickens, pigs, and other animals.

Researchers have pointed to the rising level of chemical additives in the food supply, such as those shown in this food label, as being at least a partial cause of the rise in allergies.

OYBEAN OIL, PALM OIL, PARTIALLY HYDROG
L, PARTIALLY HYDROGENATED COTTONSEED OIL, AND
OIL WITH TBHQ AND CITRIC ACID ADDED TO P
HIGH FRUCTOSE CORN SYRUP, CONTAINS TWO
FOOD STARCH – MODIFIED, SKIM MILK, LEAV
PYROPHOSPHATE, MONOCALCIUM PHOSPHAT
YCERIDES, SALT, SORBIC ACID (TO PRESERVE
ARTIFICIAL FLAVORS, PROPYLENE GLYCOL MON
UR, SOY LECITHIN, XANTHAN GUM, AGAR, NUTM

The food industry insists that all the chemicals they use are safe, and they point out that their production methods enable them to offer huge quantities of good-tasting food to American consumers at generally low prices. Many scientists, doctors, and consumers, though, believe that industrial food production has resulted in an increase in outbreaks of food-borne illness—sickness from germs and bacteria that get passed through food. Some observers also express concern that the chemicals added to our food might be contributing to public health problems ranging from early puberty to higher rates of cancer.

Finally, some people worry that modern food industry practices are contributing to the rising percentage of people with food allergies. "Modern food processing," explains *Science News,* "alters natural proteins and adds nonfood substances never before consumed in large amounts."[17]

Critics believe that the government agencies that oversee the safety of our food supply, like the Food and Drug Administration (FDA), should pay more attention to the role that food additives could be playing in rising rates of food allergy and other public health problems. "It is entirely possible that the cumulative effect of eating like this over a generation or so has caused more people to become sensitive to food," writes Eliza Meyer, who raised two children with food allergies. "While the FDA releases its umpteenth report on the dangers of fat in the American diet, consider that everyone might be missing the point entirely. What difference does fat make when your body is being forced to digest chemicals it was never intended to?"[18]

Better Reporting of Food Allergies

Some researchers believe that the rise in food allergy cases over the last two decades might be due at least in part to a better understanding of the problem. According to advocates of this theory, today's doctors, teachers, and parents simply have a greater awareness of how to recognize food allergy symptoms than they did with earlier generations.

If this theory is true, then research studies may have underestimated how many children and adults suffered from food allergies in earlier times. "A couple of decades ago, it

Food Allergies Inspire a Love for Baking

Going through your teenage years with severe food allergies is a challenge. Some teens, however, have found that such challenges can also bring opportunities. Sixteen-year-old Emma, who is allergic to tree nuts, admits that "when I was younger, class parties at school were a drag because I could never eat the food. A table in the classroom would be piled high with brownies, cookies, cupcakes, and other delectable goodies that I would not be able to enjoy because either each treat contained nuts or its label read 'Manufactured in a facility that also produces peanuts and tree nuts' in big, bold letters."

For a while Emma felt sad, left out, and different. Eventually, however, she decided that she possessed the power to change her attitude. She approached her mother and asked to learn how to bake homemade nut-free cakes and other treats at home. Emma calls this the perfect solution, because "I got to spend time with my mom while learning a new skill. Pretty soon, I found myself baking not just for class parties, but for friends, family, neighbors, and anyone else who needed a little pick-me-up. The looks on their faces after sampling one of my cookies or brownies gave me such a great sense of accomplishment and satisfaction that I was always encouraged to get back in the kitchen and keep creating."

Emma developed such a love for baking that she is considering a career as a baker or pastry chef. She even thinks about opening a fancy big-city bakery some day. "What began as a way to enjoy class parties and accommodate my food allergy has become my dream and my passion," she says.

Food Allergy and Anaphylaxis Network. "When Life Gives You Lemons: Food Allergies in the Real World," 2006. www.faanteen.org/personalstories/life_lemons.php.

Emma changed her attitude about her food allergies by baking nonallergenic cupcakes, cookies, and other pastries. She is thinking about becoming a baker.

was not uncommon to have kids sick all the time and we just said 'They have a weak stomach' or 'They're sickly,'"[19] says Anne Munoz-Furlong, founder of the Food Allergy and Anaphylaxis Network (FAAN).

According to Munoz-Furlong and others, today's parents are more aware that food allergies are a possible source of health problems. As a result, they are more likely to take their kids to allergists to see whether food allergies are the source of their stomachaches, rashes, and runny noses. These specialists have also become more likely to pass their findings along to researchers. This combination of factors might cause researchers to draw the conclusion that food allergies are rising when, in reality, only *reports* of food allergies are rising.

The Hygiene Hypothesis

Most food allergy experts doubt, however, that greater awareness of food allergies is the only factor in the soaring rates of food allergy diagnoses. They believe that other factors are at work, possibly including the so-called "hygiene hypothesis." According to this explanation, our personal hygiene—cleanliness and reduced exposure to germs—has greatly improved as vaccines, antibacterial hand soaps, airtight windows and doors, and other features of modern life have been introduced. But all of these germ-fighting innovations might be making it harder for our immune systems to develop in the way that they used to. "We could be too clean!" declares a writer for *Weekly Reader*. "Kids today come in contact with fewer germs than their grandparents did. That's in part because more medicine is available. It's also because kids get vaccines to ward off, or prevent, illnesses such as the measles. Because our immune systems have fewer germs to fight, they can get confused. Without bad bacteria to battle, they attack other things, such as milk and peanuts, instead."[20]

Today, children's reduced exposure to germs, due to vaccinations, antibacterial hand soaps, and other germ-fighting products, may be making it harder for their immune systems to develop.

Scientists have conducted a number of studies that seem to support this theory. For example, researchers have learned that children who grow up on farms, where they have constant contact with germ-carrying livestock and associated facilities, are less likely to develop allergies. Studies also indicate that children who attend day care—where lots of other germ-carrying kids can be found—are less likely to develop allergic reactions to food or other allergens. Kalb even found research that suggests that "kids born by Caesarean section . . . could be at higher risk for allergies, perhaps because they were never exposed to healthy bacteria in their mothers' birth canals. Without hard-core adversaries, the theory goes, the immune system starts battling the innocuous [harmless]—egg or wheat—instead."[21]

Some allergists believe that food allergy rates will continue to worsen as our germ-fighting technologies get even more effective and sophisticated in the years to come. As Graham Rook, a distinguished British immunologist, points out, the world we live in today is far different than the one that belonged to our ancient ancestors. "Some people had eczema [rashes] and asthma-type allergies even when we lived in the mud," he says. "But another subset has developed allergies recently, and in fact, no one knows where it will stop. My guess is that the numbers of people afflicted will get a lot worse."[22]

Genetics and Food Allergies

Researchers have also determined that there is a strong hereditary factor in food allergies. In other words, studies indicate that parents with food allergies and other kinds of allergies frequently pass food allergies on to their children. According to some estimates, the chances that a child will develop food

Researchers point to the fact that Asian and African children eat peanuts and related products from a very young age as being the reason peanut allergies are rare in those parts of the world.

Children with Food Allergies Are More Likely to Have Asthma or Other Allergic Conditions

Percentage of children under age eighteen years with asthma or other reported allergic conditions in the previous months, by reported food allergy status: United States, 2007.

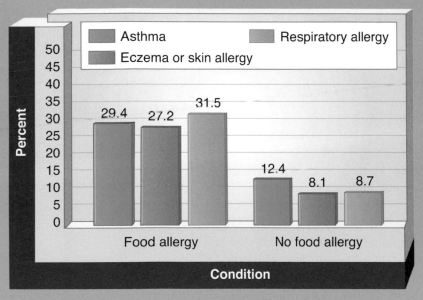

Taken from: CDC/NCHS. National Health Interview Survey. www.cdc.gov/nchs/data/databriefs/db10.htm

allergies are 30 to 50 percent higher if he or she has a parent with food allergies. If both parents have food allergies, the chances that they will pass on food allergies are even higher. Some studies indicate that kids with two food-allergenic parents are as much as 75 percent more likely to have food allergies than kids whose parents do not have food allergies.

Scientists note, however, that specific food allergies are not always passed on from parents to child. Instead, allergenic parents simply pass along genes that make their child more vulnerable to food allergies in general. For example, if a father is allergic to shellfish, his daughter may not be allergic

A Link Between Nursing and Food Allergies?

There has been a lot of debate in recent years about whether it is a good idea for mothers to avoid eating certain foods while breast-feeding their newborns. Some doctors and researchers have stated that nursing mothers who avoid highly allergenic foods might be able to reduce the likelihood that their children develop food allergies. Other allergists and scientists, however, believe that restricting the diet of a nursing mother will have no impact on her child's allergy risk.

The American Academy of Pediatrics (AAP), which is a distinguished organization of pediatricians, has taken the stance that restricting one's diet while breast-feeding is generally not necessary. The organization has even cautioned nursing mothers that some dietary restrictions—such as avoiding milk consumption, for example—could deprive their child of valuable nutrients. Even the AAP, though, has recommended that expectant mothers with a strong family history of food allergies consider avoiding peanuts, one of the most highly allergenic of all foods, during the late stages of pregnancy.

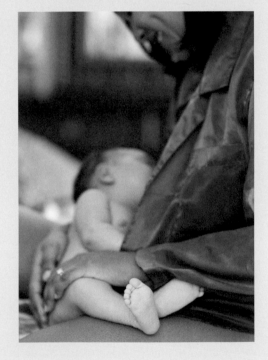

The American Academy of Pediatrics has said that restricting one's diet while breast-feeding is not necessary, but instead it recommends that nursing mothers continue drinking milk because it passes on valuable nutrients to their child.

to shellfish. She is more likely, though, to develop an allergy to peanuts or milk or wheat than a kid whose father has no food allergies at all. Given this reality, doctors urge parents who have food allergies to watch very closely the first few times they give their child a potentially allergenic food.

Weighing the Various Risk Factors

Finally, some food allergy researchers believe that parents who delay introducing some foods to their children actually place them at higher risk of developing allergies to those food items. They point out that in much of Asia and Africa, for example, children typically eat peanuts and peanut-related products from a very young age. Yet peanut allergies are extremely rare in these parts of the world. Meanwhile, in countries like the United States, where doctors and public health authorities have advocated limiting childhood exposure to peanuts, peanut allergy numbers are on the rise.

Most scientists who study food allergies have concluded, however, that there is not one single culprit responsible for the jump in food allergy rates. They believe that a combination of factors is involved. If so, then individuals and families whose lives have been affected by food allergies need to adopt a dietary approach that takes all potential factors into consideration.

CHAPTER 3

Diagnosing Food Allergies

ngelisa Keeling is a mother in Texas with three children who had been diagnosed with multiple food allergies. Preparing family meals was a daunting task for Keeling. Diagnosing food allergies can be complicated. Tests are not 100 percent accurate and sometimes people develop or overcome allergies over time. For breakfast, lunch, and dinner each day, Keeling had to come up with recipes that did not include nuts, eggs, beef, wheat, peas, and rice. As she told the *New York Times,* all of these foods were on the family kitchen's banned list because one or more or her kids were allergic to them.

Eventually, however, Keeling learned that mealtime did not have to be quite such a chore. When she took her children to allergy specialists in Colorado, they received a new series of sophisticated tests, including a procedure known as an oral food challenge test. After processing all the results, the allergists confirmed that Keeling's children did have allergies to popular foods like milk, eggs, and peanuts. Those foods still needed to be kept out of her home.

The allergists also announced, however, that the kids had shown no allergic reactions to a wide range of foods that had been considered off-limits for years. They told Keeling, for example, that her youngest son was now free to eat bananas,

beef, peas, rice, corn, and wheat, all of which had been cleared as allergens. This news was a big relief to Keeling, who admitted that "his diet had become so restricted that nutrition had become a real concern. . . . [Wheat's] the big one. Wheat is in everything, so it makes life a whole lot easier."[23]

A ten-year-old boy takes part in a double-blind oral food challenge to test for food allergies. The boy will eat a variety of foods while being watched for allergic reactions by a doctor.

Launching the Investigation

In many instances, doctors do not have much difficulty figuring out what food allergies a patient has. If a person gets hives, a runny nose, or diarrhea whenever he or she consumes dairy products, it is pretty likely that a milk allergy is the culprit. In many cases, people suffering from food allergies do not even need a medical professional to figure out which foods they should avoid. This is especially true in cases where the allergic reaction is severe. Allergist William E. Walsh uses the example of a man who eats shrimp at a restaurant: "Suddenly his eyes swell and tears flow, his nasal passages close, his skin erupts with angry red hives, and his air passage swells, threatening to strangle him. The reaction is dramatic, frightening,

FOOD FACT

Six and a half million Americans—about 2.3 percent of the general population—are allergic to seafood.

and dangerous. Obvious cause—shrimp. Obvious response—no more shrimp!"[24]

In many other cases, however, the exact nature of the problem can be a little more of a mystery. "Most foods have more than one ingredient," points out the KidsHealth.org website, "so if a kid has shrimp with peanut sauce, what's causing the allergy—the peanut sauce or the shrimp?"[25]

The task of accurately diagnosing food allergies is made more challenging by the fact that some symptoms do not reveal themselves until twelve, twenty-four, or even forty-eight hours after the food has been consumed. If you break out in hives, get watery eyes, or develop an upset stomach immediately after eating, it is pretty easy to figure out that you might have a food allergy to something in the meal you just consumed. When you have what is known as a slow-developing or delayed food reaction, though, diagnosis can be more difficult. "I suffered for years because my allergy [to corn and foods with high acidity] got missed or lost in the shuffle," says a woman named Joanne.

> Although my diarrhea occurred soon after I ate foods, my doctor never thought it might be food allergy. He also did not think that my headaches, chest tightness, or joint swelling and stiffness might be delayed reactions to foods. I found it hard to believe that I could react to something that I ate two days ago. Everybody has this misconception that food allergy always happens quickly after you eat and that if you do not suffer right after the meal, it's not allergy. This thought is wrong, and it wasn't until I changed my diet that I started to feel better.[26]

Delayed allergic reactions to food usually occur only after you have reached a certain level of consumption of the food in question. If you only eat the allergenic food once in a while, or in very low quantities, then the symptoms may not appear, or they may show up in only mild form.

Specialists also note that some food and nonfood allergens can trigger both immediate and delayed symptoms.

"For instance," writes allergist William E. Walsh, "Karen knows that popcorn makes her nose stuff up while she eats it—an immediate symptom. It also makes her stomach churn and ache many hours later—a delayed symptom."[27]

Medical professionals have a range of tools at their disposal to determine what kind of food allergies a person might

Adult-Onset Food Allergies

Most allergies—including food allergies—first show up during childhood. Sometimes, though, adults can suddenly develop an allergy to foods they have enjoyed all their lives without experiencing any problems. In some cases, a food allergy can develop virtually overnight. "You may have always been able to eat hazelnuts, and then suddenly you could develop hives on your body after eating a chocolate bar with hazelnuts," says Sami Bahna, chief of the Allergy/Immunology Section at the Louisiana State University Health Sciences Center. Some people also develop asthma for the first time in adulthood. Cases of adult-onset asthma may or may not be caused by food allergies.

Scientists are not really sure why some people can go their whole lives eating a food and then suddenly develop an allergic reaction to it. They note, though, that it is a relatively rare phenomenon.

A woman takes a skin-prick screening test for allergens. The Food Allergy and Anaphylaxis Network recommends that allergy tests not be done at home but by licensed professionals.

According to researchers, an allergy to shellfish is the most frequent type of food allergy that crops up in adulthood.

Tara Rummell Berson. "Food Allergies: What You Don't Know Can Hurt You." *Redbook*, April 2006.

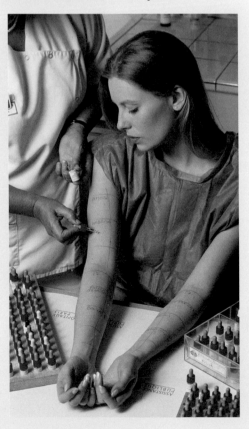

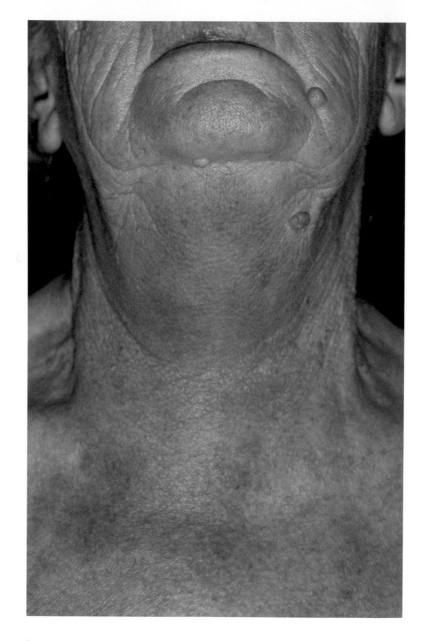

Accurately diagnosing food allergies can be challenging because the symptoms, such as this woman's swollen neck, often do not appear until twelve to forty-eight hours after the allergy-causing food is consumed.

have. Options for diagnosis include skin tests and blood tests, elimination diets, oral food challenges, and detailed surveys of personal and family medical histories. Most allergists turn to some combination of these tools to diagnose exactly what type of food or foods are causing allergy problems for their patients. In addition, some of these same tests can be useful in identifying food intolerances.

Personal and Family Medical Histories

As the first step in diagnosing potential food allergies, doctors will typically ask patients a number of questions about past episodes of sickness or discomfort that might be related to food allergies. According to the National Institute for Allergy and Infectious Diseases (NIAID), these questions should always be asked and answered fully:

- What are your symptoms?
- Can you identify particular foods that might be causing these symptoms?
- Has this food caused these symptoms on more than one occasion?
- How much of the food did you eat when the symptoms occurred?
- How was the food cooked or otherwise prepared?
- How long after you consumed the food did your symptoms begin to show?
- How long did the symptoms last?
- Have you ever eaten the suspected food without having any negative health effects?
- Were other potential triggers at work when you ate the food? (Exercise, alcohol, aspirin, and anti-inflammatory drugs can sometimes bring about similar symptoms.)
- Have you ever had these symptoms at a time when you did not consume the suspected food?
- What treatment have you received in the past when these symptoms have appeared?

Allergists also like to start their treatment by finding out more about the patient's family medical history. Scientists note, for example, that people with food allergies have a greater likelihood of having children who also have food allergies (though not necessarily the same allergies). Once the allergist has this important personal history in hand, he or she can begin the process of food allergy testing.

Skin and Blood Tests

Allergists frequently rely on skin tests and blood tests to gauge whether their patients have food allergies. In the case

The Importance of Allergy Testing

In August 2009 legendary skateboarder Andy Kessler died at age forty-nine within minutes of being stung by a wasp. The tragic incident occurred on Long Island, New York, where Kessler had been helping a friend build a deck. Food allergy organizations responded to this news by extending condolences to Kessler's family and friends—and by emphasizing how important it is for people who suspect that they might have allergies to seek professional help.

"Allergy testing, whether for environmental items, for stinging insect venom, or for foods, should be arranged through a qualified licensed medical professional, and all tests should be interpreted by a licensed medical professional with specialized training," states the Food Allergy and Anaphylaxis Network. "FAAN does not recommend allergy testing online or at home. Allergy testing can result in both false positives, and false negatives, and these can only be interpreted by a licensed medical professional."

FAAN. "Death by Insect Renews Importance for Allergy Testing." Food Allergy and Anaphylaxis Network. www.foodallergy.org/page/death-by-insect-renews-importance-for-allergy-testing.

of skin tests, the allergist pricks or scrapes the skin of the patient with a device soaked in a liquid version, or extract, of the food being tested. If the scraped area has an allergic reaction, such as reddening or noticeable raising of the skin, over the next ten to fifteen minutes, it is an indication that the patient's body has generated immunoglobulin E (IgE). IgE antibodies are produced by the body's immune system to fight off unhealthy germs, but they are also created when the immune system mistakenly identifies a food as a threat. If an allergist sees a positive IgE result, he or she can then flag the food being tested as a potential allergy source. Allergists can test for dozens of food allergies at a time using skin tests.

If a skin test for a specific food comes up negative, then the patient generally does not have to worry about being allergic to that food. Positive skin tests for food allergies can be misleading, however. Even when a skin test reveals the presence of IgE antibodies, it does not mean that the person will have an allergic reaction when eating that food. In some cases, the amount of IgE antibodies generated in response to a food is high enough to provoke a positive skin test result—but low enough to allow the person to eat that food without any negative reaction. This phenomenon is known as a false positive.

Allergists also make use of blood tests to check for food allergies. Like skin tests, blood tests measure the presence of IgE antibodies. They are effective in ruling out some foods that do not trigger the production of IgE antibodies. These tests have the same potential for false positives as skin tests, though. In 2010, in fact, the NIAID estimated that 50 to 90 percent of food allergies detected through skin and blood

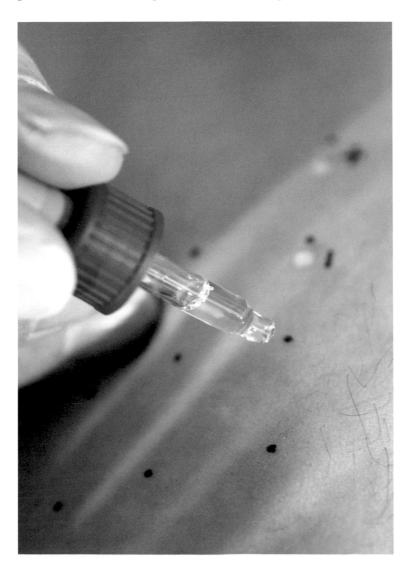

A medical worker applies a solution soaked in an extract of the food being tested to the arm of a patient undergoing a skin-prick allergy test. If a reddening or noticeable raising of the skin occurs within fifteen minutes, it is an indication that the patient is allergic.

testing are actually false positives. "The results of these tests," emphasizes the NIAID, "only show that you produce IgE antibodies to food allergens. Blood and skin tests alone cannot be used to diagnose food allergy."[28]

This does not mean that skin and blood testing for food allergies is worthless. It just means that allergists and their patients need to recognize that the results of these tests are more reliable and better understood if other testing procedures are used as well.

Elimination Diets

Some allergists make use of a test known as the elimination diet. With this method of allergy detection, patients completely eliminate common allergens (such as eggs, wheat, corn, and dairy products) and suspected allergens from their diet. "And eliminate means completely," writes Elisa Meyer. "The diet will have no validity if you allow even the smallest amount of any of these foods to be eaten."[29] After faithfully following the elimination diet for a period of time—usually two weeks—the patient gradually reintroduces these foods one at a time. This process serves to link allergy symptoms to specific foods. Once the allergenic foods have been identified, this information can be used to put together a diet plan for the person with food allergies.

Many allergists and physicians regard elimination diet tests as a useful tool. They caution, however, that the diets are best used in combination with other allergy detection methods. People with a history of severe allergic food reactions should not be tested through elimination dieting due to the risk that such a reaction may occur when a food is reintroduced. In addition, it can be hard to pinpoint food allergies through this method. Some studies indicate that elimination diets remove broad categories of food without sufficient evidence that they cause allergic reactions. "We get patients referred to us all the time who have been placed on very restrictive diets. They may be off

FOOD FACT

Boys are more likely to develop food allergies than girls.

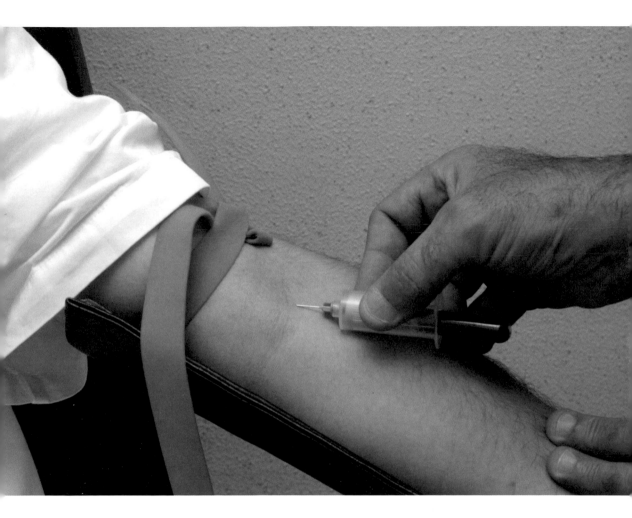

ten or twenty foods," says allergist Hugh Sampson. "We go through a full evaluation, and it turns out they are allergic to only one or two."[30]

Overly restrictive elimination diets can also make it harder for patients to get the vitamins and nutrients that they need. This is especially true of children, whose food choices are dictated by concerned parents.

Allergists also use blood tests to measure the amount of IgE antibodies that are present. But 50 to 90 percent of skin and blood tests give false positives.

Oral Food Challenges

Oral food challenges are widely seen among allergists as a particularly useful test for food allergies. The steps involved in an oral food challenge are simple and straightforward. First, patients are given extremely small doses of a food that

There are three types of oral food challenges available: (1) An open food challenge, (2) a single-blind challenge, and (3) the most effective one, a double-blind placebo-controlled challenge.

is suspected of triggering allergic reactions. As the patient consumes the food sample, an allergist watches closely to see whether any negative response occurs. The patient and allergist then move on to the next suspected allergy source and conduct the same process.

There are three types of oral food challenge tests. Under an open food challenge test, both the patient and the doctor know which specific food is being tested. Under a single-blind food challenge test, the doctor know what food the patient is receiving, but the patient does not. The best—and most expensive—of the oral challenge tests is the double-blind

placebo-controlled food challenge, or DBPCFC. In this test, neither the doctor nor the patient knows whether the patient is consuming a suspected food allergen or a harmless substance (known as a placebo).

The allergist, though, still has a very important role. He or she determines the starting dose for each suspected allergen based on the patient's medical history. The allergist also decides whether to increase the dosage and determines how long each dose should be monitored for delayed reaction. The allergy expert also has to interpret the results of the oral food challenge and make dietary recommendations that will keep the patient in good health.

Allergists say that oral food challenges—and especially the DBPCFC version—are the most reliable food allergy testing procedures available. Studies seem to confirm this viewpoint. In 2010, for example, the *Journal of Pediatrics* published a study involving a group of Denver, Colorado, schoolchildren who had been classified as food-allergic. After these children took oral challenges, they were able to resume eating about 90 percent of the foods that had previously been declared off-limits because of skin tests and blood tests.

The big problems with oral food challenges are that they are expensive, time consuming, and can provoke anxiety among young test takers. In addition, most oral food challenges are undertaken by allergy experts and researchers rather than ordinary physicians, so the waiting lists for taking the test are often long.

Finding Peace with a Diagnosis

For many people, being diagnosed with food allergies—especially severe ones—can be a difficult development. They may feel deep disappointment that they can no longer eat foods they have long enjoyed, or anger that they have to worry about whether their favorite restaurant will be able to accommodate their special dietary needs. Some people who grow up with food allergies or develop them in adulthood may understandably feel that the whole thing is just "not fair."

In some cases, however, people who are diagnosed with food allergies actually feel a sense of relief. This can be especially true of people who learn about their food allergies later in life. For these individuals, learning the source of long-standing stomach problems, rashes, tingling lips and tongue, and other symptoms can give them a renewed sense of freedom and control. Once they have a diagnosis in hand, their health problems are no longer a mystery to them. Instead, they can make plans and develop strategies that allow them to keep their food allergies at bay as they go about their daily lives.

CHAPTER **4**

Scientists, Lawmakers, and Food Makers Respond

B oth the U.S. government and America's scientific and medical communities have developed a wide range of policies and programs to respond to food allergies. Some of these efforts focus on reaching a better understanding of how food allergies work and how they can be effectively treated or prevented. Others are more concerned with helping people with food allergies safely navigate through the world of food. These policies and programs are closely monitored by numerous consumer advocacy organizations devoted to the issue of food allergies. Groups like the Food Allergy and Anaphylaxis Network (FAAN) and the Asthma and Allergy Foundation (AAF) are important sources of information and support for families dealing with the challenge of food allergies.

Important Laws for People with Food Allergies

The first major law affecting individuals with food allergies was the Rehabilitation Act of 1973. This law was not written specifically for people with allergies, but it still had a

President George H.W. Bush signs the Americans with Disabilities Act into law in 1990. Under the ADA, establishments that provide food to children made changes to their procedures to better accommodate those with food allergies.

considerable impact on them. The Rehabilitation Act was designed to protect individuals with physical or mental disabilities from discrimination in schools and the workplace. One provision of the Rehabilitation Act, known as Section 504, was particularly important for people suffering from food allergies. Section 504 declared that school districts had to keep elementary and secondary school children with disabilities integrated in regular school activities whenever possible. It also directed schools to provide disabled students with an equal opportunity to participate in extracurricular activities like band or sports.

After the Rehabilitation Act was passed into law, school administrators worked with parents of disabled children all across the country to develop Section 504 plans that would ensure that students with disabilities could have a safe and fair school experience. Some kids with food allergies benefited as well, even though people did not always think of their allergies as a disability. "A 504 plan works well for children with food allergies because it can address lunchroom and classroom policies, general food and hand-washing policies, field trip protocol, and emergency procedures if there is an allergic reaction," explains attorney Tess O'Brien-Heinzen. "Unfortunately, many schools do not regularly evaluate food allergy sufferers under the rubric of the Rehabilitation Act but rather attempt to deal with food allergies on a more informal case-by-case basis."[31]

The next major federal law that had an impact on people with food allergies was the Americans with Disabilities Act (ADA). Passed in 1990, the ADA was the nation's first comprehensive civil rights law for people with disabilities. It required employers, businesses, schools, and government agencies to make sure that they operated in a way that did not discriminate against people with disabilities. Many establishments for children that provide food as part of their services—such as schools, child-care centers, and summer camps—made changes to their operations so as to better meet the needs of children with food allergies under the ADA.

As it turned out, though, the U.S. court system did not necessarily believe that either Section 504 or the ADA applied to people with food allergies. To be protected under the ADA, for example, "an individual must prove that he or she is disabled," writes O'Brien-Heinzen. "This has not been an easy task. Courts have tended to interpret the term narrowly; indeed, individuals with such serious illnesses as AIDS, cancer, and diabetes have been among those found not to have disabilities under the ADA and therefore to not be covered by its protections."[32]

In 1999 the U.S. Eighth Circuit Court decided in the case *Land v. Baptist Medical Center* that a day-care center did not have to make special accommodations for a food-allergic preschooler. The Court ruled that even though the preschooler was severely allergic to peanut products, she did not qualify for ADA protection because she could eat other foods safely and could breathe normally except when she was around peanuts and peanut-related foods.

This ruling surprised and outraged families dealing with severe food allergies, but it remained the law of the land for

In 2008 President George W. Bush signed into law the Americans with Disabilities Act Amendments Act. The legislation greatly expanded the meaning of the term disabilities *to include severe food allergies.*

the next several years. In 2008, though, Congress passed and President George W. Bush signed into law the Americans with Disabilities Act Amendments Act (ADAAA). This legislation greatly expanded the meaning of the term *disability* in the original Americans with Disabilities Act and the Rehabilitation Act. It states that the definition of disability should be "construed in favor of broad coverage of individuals." Legal experts believe that this new language makes it much easier for people with food allergies (and other people with mental or physical impairments) to qualify as disabled under the law and receive its protections. Schools and other establishments now have a greater legal obligation to make sure that their facilities are safe and inclusive for children and adults who have food allergies.

Food Safety Through Labeling and Instruction

In addition to the Rehabilitation Act, the ADA, and the ADAAA, lawmakers in Washington have passed two other major laws pertaining to food allergies in recent years. In

Banning Peanuts in School

Some of the most severe allergic food reactions come from peanuts. With the number of cases of anaphylactic shock from peanut allergens steadily rising, many school districts have decided to limit or ban peanuts on their campuses. In some cases, administrators have established peanut-free rooms or cafeteria tables. In others, they have approved complete bans on having peanuts or peanut-related products anywhere on school grounds.

These measures have prompted complaints from some parents. Moms and dads with finicky eaters say that outlawing peanut butter and jelly sandwiches makes it even harder for them to pack nutritious lunches that their children will eat. The majority of parents and students, though, seem to understand that these bans are necessary. As one parent told *Weekly Reader*, "All kids have a right to be safe in school, and that's something all kids should care about. If by giving up a food you like, you could keep a classmate from getting sick, why wouldn't you want to?"

In addition to instituting peanut butter bans, a few school districts have begun to train teachers, bus drivers, cafeteria workers, and other school employees about how to use epinephrine autoinjectors, which are typically carried by kids with severe allergies. These medical devices inject doses of epinephrine (or adrenaline), a medicine that helps the body ward off the negative effects of allergic reactions. Most states still only allow school nurses to inject epinephrine into students, but the U.S. Congress has begun weighing bills that would allow schoolteachers and other faculty members to do so.

School districts have also made special efforts to educate kids about the risks of severe food allergies. The state of Connecticut, for example, requires teachers to educate their classes about allergies. Supporters believe that these measures not only keep kids with food allergies safer, but also help increase peer support and understanding.

"Peanut Butter Jam: Will Food Allergies Kick Your Favorite Snack out of School?" *Weekly Reader (WR), Senior Edition,* October 10, 2008, p. 4.

Because peanuts can cause life-threatening allergic reactions in severely allergic students, many school districts have now banned their presence on campus or have created peanut-free cafeterias and vending areas.

FOOD FACT

A 2007 survey by the School Nutrition Association found that 18 percent of U.S. schools had some type of peanut ban in place.

2004 Congress passed the Food Allergen Labeling and Consumer Protection Act (FALCPA), which went into effect in 2006. This law requires food manufacturers to clearly label any packaged foods that have ingredients with proteins from any of the eight major allergen categories—milk, egg, wheat, peanuts, soybeans, tree nuts, fish, and shellfish. FALCPA also insists that these warning labels be written so that they are easy for consumers to understand. Advocates for families dealing with food allergy issues praised the law for making food shopping easier for millions of people with allergies to milk, peanuts, wheat, eggs, and other foods.

In January 2011 the Food Allergy and Anaphylaxis Management Act (FAAMA) was signed into law by President Barack Obama. The law, which was passed as part of a broad set of new national food safety laws and food production regulations, was written in large part by members of FAAN. Its passage marked the end of a long struggle for FAAN and other advocates for people with food allergies. Although FAAMA had first been introduced in Congress in 2005 and had support from both Democrats and Republicans, it never managed to get enacted until 2011.

FAAMA is designed to provide schools across the country with the resources they need to protect students with food allergies. FAAMA authorized the federal government to create voluntary, national guidance materials for managing food allergies in the nation's schools. One of the bill's leading champions was Senator Christopher Dodd, a Democrat from Connecticut whose daughter has been diagnosed with severe food allergies. "All of our nation's children deserve a safe and healthy learning environment," says Dodd. "As a parent of a child who suffers from severe food allergies, I know firsthand the distress this can cause young children and their families. As the number of children with food allergies continues to rise, FAAMA will establish guidelines for the management of food allergies in schools—protecting the well-being of millions of children with life-threatening allergies."[33]

In addition to these federal laws, some states have passed regulations to protect their citizens from exposure to food allergies. In February 2010, for example, Massachusetts passed a law requiring twenty-four thousand restaurants across the state to educate their staffs about food allergies. The law also required restaurants to post information and instructions about food allergies in a staff area.

Seeking a Cure for Food Allergies

Scientists have developed a variety of drugs that help people deal with allergic reactions, but they have yet to find a sure-fire cure for food allergies. Researchers at government, university, and corporate laboratories, though, are working diligently to discover treatments that might free people from the hovering threat of food allergies. Some research programs are also focused on finding ways to prevent future generations from ever developing food allergies in the first place.

A scientist examines cell cultures for reactions. Immunotherapy involves tinkering with the immune system so it changes its behavior; for example, toward an allergen.

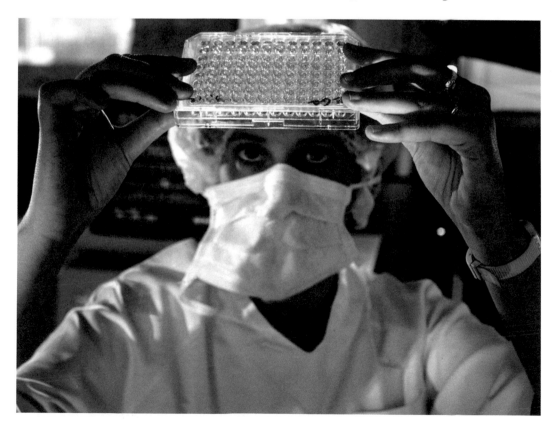

One of the most promising of these areas of study is called immunotherapy. This process involves tinkering with the immune system so that it changes its behavior. Immunotherapy is already being used with a fair amount of success for treating other types of allergies, like hay fever. Some forms of immunotherapy have even been used as part of cancer treatments. In the case of food allergies, scientists are trying to retrain food-allergic immune systems so that they no longer "freak out" when those foods enter the body, whether by eating, touching, or breathing in particles.

For food allergies, the immunotherapy process involves giving allergic people extremely tiny amounts of the food to which they are allergic. The researchers then very gradually increase the dose of the food the patients receive. This process takes place under extremely close medical supervision in the case of any severe allergic reaction. In some of these tests, people with food allergies have shown an increased ability to consume foods that have always given them severe problems in the past. This has been true even of people suffering from allergies to eggs and peanuts, which are notorious for triggering serious health problems such as anaphylaxis attacks.

Researchers admit that they do not know how far they will be able to go with this line of study. There are indications, for example, that allergy immunotherapy may only work if participants receive the therapy on a daily or almost daily basis. Otherwise, the allergic reactions intensify again, and all the earlier progress that the patient made is lost.

Nonetheless, many allergists are extremely excited about the treatment advances they have already made. "I think we're all encouraged that progress has happened relatively quickly," says Robert Wood, an allergy specialist at Johns Hopkins Children's Center in Baltimore.

> If nothing else, the experiments have shown for the first time that curing food allergies is at least possible. . . . Some children who began studies with immune reactions to even the smallest trace of peanut can now eat up to 13 nuts in one sitting. Similar dramatic gains have been seen for milk and egg allergies. Only a few children have been involved in each study so far, but researchers are cautiously increasing the number of enrollees.[34]

Allergists are investigating other approaches as well in their quest to free people from food allergies. For example, scientists are experimenting with genetic food allergy vaccines, also sometimes called DNA immunizations. Under this program, a scientist might create a vaccine for peanut

Hoping for a Cure

Millions of families who have members with severe food allergies wish for a cure every day. Christine, for example, has spent most of her daughter's life working around her extremely severe peanut allergy. Her daughter was diagnosed with the allergy at thirteen months of age, when she ate a single bite from a peanut butter sandwich. "She immediately spit it out and developed hives around her mouth," recalls Christine. "The hives quickly spread to her eyes and they swelled up. Her entire face was so swollen that she was unrecognizable, so I gave her a teaspoon of an antihistamine and quickly called 911."

Christine's daughter recovered at the hospital, but doctors confirmed that peanuts and foods with peanut-derived ingredients posed a serious health threat to the toddler. Since then, Christine and her daughter have figured out ways to get around her allergy when she goes to school or the homes of friends. This task has been made much easier by the thoughtfulness of friends and other parents who check in with Christine to confirm which foods are safe for her daughter. Nonetheless, Christine admits that she continues to "hope and pray for a cure so that I can cross this off my list of worries as a parent."

Christine D. "A Food Allergy That Reemerged." FAAN: The Food Allergy and Anaphylaxis Network. www.foodallergy.org/page/a-food-allergy-that-reemerged.

Millions of American families have members with severe food allergies and wish for a cure every day. It is a constant struggle to ensure that allergic family members do not ingest food to which they are allergic.

allergy, for example, by injecting genes with coding for peanut protein directly into immune system cells. Such a genetic change would get the immune system cells to make the protein themselves—and remain calm when the protein comes into the body through peanut-butter cookies, peanut oil, or any other foods. "The idea behind DNA immunization is that when the body produces the allergen from within, the immune system no longer views the allergen as a foreign invader, and hence has no reason to attack it," explains Wood. "This therapy is far from ready for human experimentation, but similar strategies are being used to treat other diseases in people, including cystic fibrosis and sickle cell disease, so this may not be as far fetched as it sounds."[35]

Even the most optimistic researchers admit, though, that finding a permanent cure for food allergies will require years of additional study and experimentation. The challenge, according to journalist Claudia Kalb, is that "while scientists have a basic understanding of how allergies work, they can still be stumped by the immune system, which is too complex to submit easily to their control." For the time being, she concludes, "The best parents and children can do now is avoid the culprits"[36] that cause allergic reactions.

Changing Industry Practices to Reduce Cross-Contamination

The food industry is also making greater investments in sophisticated machinery and technology in order to minimize allergic reactions from food. Their chief concern is accidental cross-contamination, which takes place when a food item that does not itself contain any allergens becomes contaminated with an allergen at some point in the food delivery process.

Cross-contamination most frequently occurs at home or in restaurant kitchens. It usually happens when a knife, cutting board, bowl, or other kitchen implement is used to prepare an allergenic food, then comes into contact with a previously "safe" food before being washed or otherwise sanitized. The safe food thus becomes tainted with residues from the allergenic food to the point that it too can trigger health problems when it is eaten.

Food processing companies face this same challenge, except on a much bigger scale. Many food production facilities manufacture a variety of different food items that appear on supermarket shelves. If they are not careful in their operations, they can fall victim to cross-contamination as well. When this happens in a food processing facility, huge volumes of food can become contaminated with allergens in a matter of minutes. Fortunately for food makers and their customers, the industry has developed advanced systems to shield their operations from accidental contamination from food allergens.

Cross-contamination frequently occurs at home or in restaurant kitchens, but food processors have developed advanced systems to shield their operations from accidental food allergen contamination.

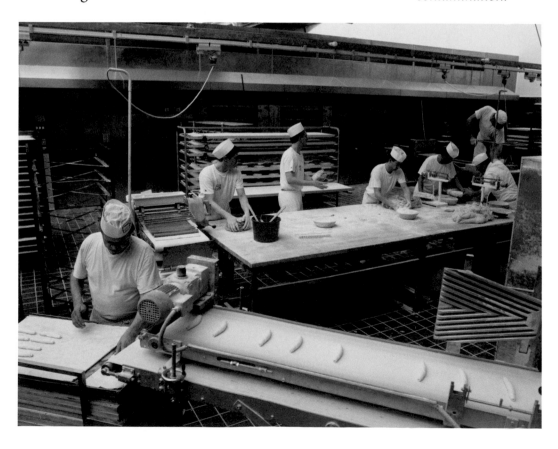

The ice cream industry is a good example. "Ice cream manufacturers typically produce both nonallergenic and allergenic products on the same [production] lines," writes Kevin T. Higgins. "They are dipping into technology's equipment arsenal to cope with the allergen-control challenge. Dreyer's Grand Ice Cream installed more than 100 mix-proof valves at its Bakersfield [California] plant to enhance its ability to clean out egg, peanut, and other allergen residues from lines before a nonallergenic product is run."[37]

Companies that avoid cross-contamination and properly label their food products can obtain significant business benefits in the long run. "It all boils down to trust," says Anne Munoz-Furlong of FAAN. "If people affected by food allergies trust the information they are given, they will trust that product, and they become very brand loyal and tell everyone else."[38]

CHAPTER **5**

Adjusting to Life

iving with food allergies can be a significant challenge, not just for the person with allergies but also for other members of the family. This is especially true in cases where the food allergies can cause severe and potentially life-threatening episodes of anaphylactic shock. Families that receive a diagnosis of severe food allergy have to make changes to virtually every aspect of daily life.

Practical matters aside, food allergies have the potential to take a heavy toll on one's social life as well. This is especially true for children and teens whose allergies are so severe that they must carry epinephrine autoinjectors with them wherever they go. Food allergies can be an additional source of friction between teens seeking independence and parents who are keenly aware of the many different ways that their child might be accidentally exposed to allergens. Food allergies can also put up walls between kids and their peers. Some classmates might resent rules that do not allow them to bring some of their favorite foods to school. Others find the idea of severe food allergies so bizarre that they avoid kids who have them, as if the condition were contagious.

Finally, food allergies can become a weapon in the hands of bullies. "In junior high and even in high school, telling everyone that you have a food allergy can be like hanging a sign on

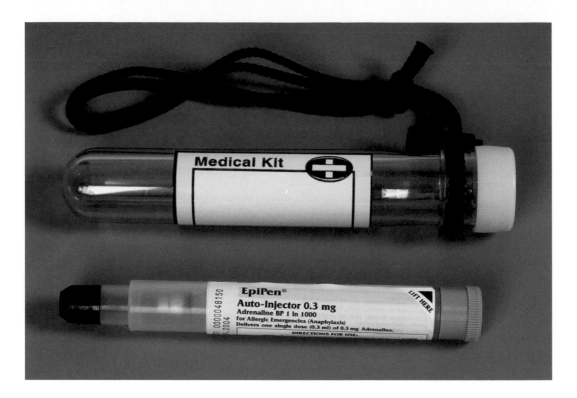

Children and teens with severe food allergies must carry an epinephrine autoinjector such as this one at all times.

your back that says 'Kick Me!'" writes allergy specialist Robert A. Wood. "Any exposed weakness is a vulnerability that the school bully may quickly pick up on and begin to exploit."[39]

Despite all these additional challenges, though, tens of thousands of kids and adults with significant food allergies are able to carve out happy and productive lives for themselves. Armed with confidence and knowledge, they march out into the world every day with a determination to keep their allergies at bay. They refuse to allow food allergies to define them or keep them from pursuing their dreams.

Food Allergies and Social Acceptance

Young children who have severe food allergies generally do not spend a lot of time worrying about whether their condition will lead to rejection from other kids in the classroom or the day-care center. The entire issue is handled by adults, and youngsters just go about the business of playing. They have no idea whether or not peanuts, milk, or other allergens are absent or handled with extreme care.

As kids get older and slip into adolescence and teenage life, though, their awareness of the wider world increases. It is here that special food rules for certain kids come to their attention. It is also during this stage of development that many adolescents and teens become extremely uncomfortable with the idea of being different from their peers in any way. They want to fit in and not draw attention to themselves. For many young people with severe food allergies, their condition thus becomes a source of embarrassment and discomfort.

In some cases, the feelings of humiliation and embarrassment over their condition can lead teens with food allergies to adopt self-destructive attitudes. "I've had patients who've literally said they'd rather die than use an EpiPen [an epinephrine autoinjector, used to counteract life-threatening allergic reactions]," says Calman Prussin, a researcher with the National Institute of Allergy and Infectious Diseases. "And I wonder: Where did they get that message?"[40]

Many adolescents and teens with food allergies are uncomfortable being different from their peers. They do not want to draw attention to their condition because of feelings of embarrassment.

Kids Who Leave Their Allergy Medication at Home

Medical studies have consistently shown that teenagers with food allergies need to be more careful about protecting themselves from potentially serious allergic reactions. In 2006, for example, a survey conducted by allergists found that many teens with a history of severe food allergies have a habit of trying food without adequately investigating whether it is safe for them.

The survey also revealed that teens with severe food allergies frequently leave their epinephrine autoinjectors at home when going out. Only 43 percent of respondents said that they took their autoinjectors with them when playing sports. About 30 percent of teens also admitted that they leave their autoinjectors at home when going to friends' homes or attending after-school activities, like dances. This behavior seems even more incredible given that fully 82 percent of the participants in the survey reported that they had suffered at least one anaphylaxis attack in the past. In addition, more than half of them reported that they had experienced three or more anaphylactic episodes.

According to Scott Sicherer of the Mount Sinai School of Medicine in New York City, allergic teens need to halt this risky behavior: "Teens have to be consistent in carrying [their epinephrine autoinjectors]. If they're wearing tight clothes, they can use a holster; if they're at a sports event, they can put it in their gym bag. Most teens always have their cell phones, so they certainly should be able to take along their medication."

"Teens with Food Allergies Take Risks." *WebMD Health News,* March 6, 2006. www .webmd.com/allergies/news/20060306/teens-food-allergies-risks.

Adopting a Positive Attitude

Some kids with severe food allergies say that their own personal attitude toward their medical condition can make a big difference in how other kids perceive them. "The number one fear for many of those who live with food allergies is not the fear of having a reaction, but the fear of being accepted," writes Annie Jorgensen, winner of the Miss Wisconsin Outstanding Teen scholarship pageant in 2011.

> It has been my personal experience that others are more accepting of your food allergy once you have accepted them yourself. I believe this is achieved when you are fully prepared and confident in any social situation. Attitude is contagious—if you are comfortable in your own skin, challenges and all, others around you will embrace your food allergies and will be open to learning how to keep you safe.[41]

Many kids with food allergies also find that their worries about being accepted by classmates and teammates are overblown. Fourteen-year-old Caitlin, for example, was very excited when she made the junior varsity (JV) volleyball team at her high school. When she realized that she would have to tell not only her JV teammates and coaches but also the varsity squad about her severe allergies to peanuts and tree nuts, though, she became extremely nervous. "I wasn't sure if they would understand [but] I knew that I had to let them know eventually and that it was important for my safety," she recalls. As it turned out, all the players and coaches were supportive. "All through the season, the team was wonderful in helping me manage my allergy on the bus, at away games, and during special events, such as senior night or team sleepovers. I was lucky to be with such a nice group of people, but also proud of myself for taking charge and keeping myself safe. . . . It opened my eyes to how considerate other teens can be about allergies."[42]

Unfortunately, some adolescents and teens learn that people are not as understanding and accepting as Caitlin's teammates and coaches were. Some kids with food allergies find that their medical condition provides an opening for bullies. Others discover to their great disappointment that their friends are not who they thought they were. The key to handling these difficult experiences is to maintain a sense of self-worth and seek out peers who will accept you for who you are, allergies and all.

Most Common Allergies in Children

Children with food allergies were most commonly allergic to:

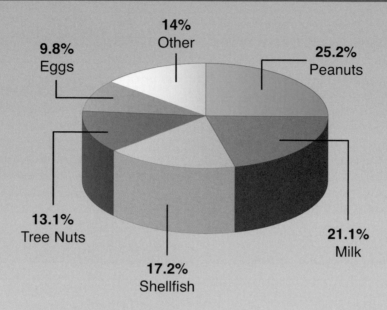

14%
Other

9.8%
Eggs

25.2%
Peanuts

13.1%
Tree Nuts

21.1%
Milk

17.2%
Shellfish

Survey results from 2011 study sponsored by the National Institute of Allergy and Infectious Diseases.

Taken from: www.childrensmemorial.org/newsroom/release06202011.aspx.

Seventeen-year-old Carlos, who is allergic to milk, wheat, eggs, peanuts, and many other foods, recalls that he endured a lot of taunting from middle school bullies. They made fun of him and even threatened to poison him. As time went on, however, Carlos says that he "learned to deal with the bullies. I realized that I am not defined by my food allergies, that there is so much more to me than what foods I can and cannot eat."[43]

Thirteen-year-old Makenna says that her food allergies actually provide her with an opportunity of sorts—to find out which of her classmates are worth knowing and befriending. "I have been left out, made fun of, threatened, mistreated, and called names [because of my allergies]," she admits. Makenna adds, though, that "I've learned not to listen to them [the bullies] and find real friends, those who help look after me, who remind me that I can't have a certain kind of yogurt at lunch, and those who understand my situation. I use to be embarrassed to carry around my epinephrine auto-injector with me at all times, but now, I accept it. It's a part of me; I was meant to have these allergies."[44]

Learning to Cook Allergen-Free Meals

For many children, teens, and adults with food allergies, one of the biggest challenges they face is how to find food that is both tasty and safe to eat outside the home. Whereas people without food allergies can go anywhere and eat anything without worrying for their safety, the stakes for food allergy sufferers are far higher. As journalist Mary Brophy Marcus observes, for people with food allergies, "dining out, eating in other people's homes, and munching at office parties and school events can be a minefield. One bite of the wrong cupcake or cookie and a person could face days of illness, lost work or worse—anaphylactic shock."[45]

Some families and individuals that have to deal with serious and multiple food allergies limit their exposure to foods outside of the home. They either eat virtually all their meals at home or bring their own prepared food with them wherever they go. Allergists say that in some of the most severe food allergy cases involving children who are still learning about allergy triggers in foods, these precautions are not only sensible but almost necessary.

It is worth noting, however, that dietary options for people with food allergies have expanded greatly in recent years. Entire cookbooks and websites are now devoted to making allergen-free meals and desserts. In addition, food manufacturers have noticed the rising number of people

FOOD FACT

Allergists confirm that there have been cases where food proteins released into the air from vapor or steam from foods being cooked have triggered allergic reactions. They note, however, that these incidents are very rare and usually occur only with fish.

Some families and individuals who have to deal with serious and multiple food allergies limit their exposure to potentially unsafe foods by eating only at home.

with food allergies over the last decade or so, and they have rushed to attract these consumers with a variety of new products. "Companies have created lots of good substitutes for favorite foods," confirms KidsHealth.org. "Everything from dairy-free mashed potatoes to wheat-free chocolate chunk cookies!"[46]

These expanded supermarket offerings have made life much easier for families grappling with food allergies. Parents with allergic kids still have to read food labels very closely to look for problem ingredients, and they admit that dealing with food allergies is a big hassle. Some of them say, though, that food shopping and meal making gets a lot easier over time.

Pete Wells recalls that when his son Dexter was diagnosed with multiple food allergies, it seemed like there were hardly any foods left that the family could make for him. "He was a year old when we learned he would have to avoid tuna, clams, and shrimp," recalls Wells. "And onions. And garlic. Peanuts, almonds, walnuts and cashews. Sesame and poppy seeds. Egg whites, chickpeas, and lentils. Soybeans and anything containing soy, which by itself put about half the supermarket off limits." As the months passed by, though, Wells and his wife got educated about food allergies, expanded their cooking horizons, and became adept at substituting ingredients. By the time Dexter was in preschool they were making eggless cupcakes, pancakes, and meatballs that were just as tasty as the traditional versions. "The strange thing," says Wells, "was how easy it was."[47]

Eating Outside the Home

For middle school and high school students, eating every meal at home is usually not a realistic option. Between classes, after-school jobs, extracurricular activities, dating, and other social events, youths with food allergies spend long periods of time far away from the familiar confines of the family kitchen.

One solution for allergic youngsters and teens (and adults) is to carry safe food items with them. But most of them also will eat out at restaurants and friends' houses. Allergists are supportive of these choices, provided that the patients take steps to ensure that the food they are eating is safe for them. For example, people with food allergies should notify wait staff of their condition, and they should not shy away from personally touching base with cooks, chefs, and other food preparers to let them know about special food requirements. "Eating out with a food allergy can be a challenge," admits eighteen-year-old Julie, who is allergic to milk and other dairy products.

> However, that should not stop you from doing so. Overall, feeling comfortable where you are is critical. If you don't get a good vibe from the people you talk to or just don't trust that the food you're getting is safe,

do not eat there. . . . Once you find a few restaurants that you feel comfortable eating at, continue eating at them. It's nice to get to know the people who work at a restaurant and develop a good relationship with them, helping you feel safe to enjoy your meal.[48]

Allergists often tell their patients that they can make the whole eating out process much easier and safer if they prepare written materials in advance that can be shared with restaurant chefs, waiters, and waitresses. These personalized cards should include all foods and related ingredients to which the person is allergic, emergency contact information, and information on ways to avoid cross-contamination of food via tainted utensils, dishes, pots, and counter surfaces in kitchen and serving areas.

These information cards can also include epinephrine autoinjector operating instructions in case an allergic reaction occurs and the victim is unable to treat himself or herself. These instructions can be lifesavers, although many people at risk of anaphylactic shock from food allergies make sure that they are accompanied by friends or family members that know how to use the syringe-like devices. "Many of my friends know where my EpiPens® are and how to use them," says sixteen-year-old Peter, who is allergic to fish, peanuts, and tree nuts. "When I go camping, my cooking partner makes sure all the food that he provides for dinner is safe. If I were to eat a nut in the middle of a week-long canoeing trip, getting help would be a challenge. . . . Although my friends help ensure my safety, ultimately I am responsible for my safety."[49]

A Whole New Set of Parenting Challenges

As kids grow older, they naturally seek more independence from their parents. Most parents recognize that they have to give their sons and daughters progressively more freedom to explore the world around them—and even to make painful mistakes sometimes. They also know more than their kids about the perils and pitfalls of growing up, though, so it is natural—and sometimes wise—for them to try to protect their adolescents and teens.

Keeping Your Guard Up When Eating Out

Thousands of people with serious food allergies eat out at restaurants without ill effects. They take the appropriate precautions, such as notifying restaurant chefs and wait staff about their allergies, and they make sure that they carry antiallergy medication with them at all times. Many families who wrestle with food allergies eventually develop favorite restaurants, where they order something from the same group of safe meals every time. If you are a person with severe allergies, such a place can come to seem like a safe haven in a world of food uncertainty.

Even after you have found a restaurant that takes your health issues seriously, though, allergists emphasize that you have to keep your guard up. This caution is especially necessary in the event that you become comfortable with a particular restaurant chain. "If you find a local restaurant where you feel safe eating, the same chain or franchise a few miles away may have different ingredients in the exact same dish that can make you sick," writes Melissa Taylor, who has grappled with food allergies all her life. "Perhaps no matter where you have gone . . . this chain has used the same ingredients and cooking practices as the others in the chain. However, you only need to have *one* that doesn't handle food preparation *exactly* the same in order to potentially experience a reaction. Never get into an attitude of complacency when eating out. Make sure you check ingredients and possible cross-contamination each and every time."

Melissa Taylor. *Food Allergy Survivors Together Handbook.* Lincoln, NE: Writers Club, 2002, p. 42.

When dining out, families and individuals should let the restaurant staff know about their food allergies.

Oftentimes the family doctor or allergist can alleviate tensions over food rules and precautions by offering advice and explaining the potential risks and rewards so the family can arrive at a reasonable consensus.

Finding the right balance between protecting and letting go is hard enough for the parents of children who do not have any serious allergy issues. Imagine how much harder it is for parents to watch their kid go out the door for a sleepover or a basketball game in a distant town when that kid is at risk of dying if he or she accidentally runs across a small smear of peanut butter or swallows a tiny amount of egg, wheat, soy, or milk.

In situations where food-allergic kids clash with their parents over food rules and precautions—such as whether they should go to a party where allergenic food might be present—it is sometimes a good idea to seek the judgment of an impartial third party. According to Wood, the family allergist is often ideally suited for this role. "Your doctor is unlikely to make the decision for you, but he may be able to defuse the emotional dynamite, highlight the facts, and explain the potential risks and rewards, so you can arrive at a more reasonable consensus," he suggests. "Some parents are far too restrictive, and teens are far too prone to taking risks. The trick is to find a happy medium."[50]

Allergists also frequently urge their younger patients to try to understand what their parents are going through. Many parents of children with severe food allergies say that their lives are never the same after the diagnosis. Since scientists believe that food allergies seem to be passed down at least in some cases through heredity, parents sometimes struggle with feelings of guilt. Others find that they no longer have time for long-treasured hobbies or friendships because they spend so much of their time keeping kids safe from food allergens.

Finding Understanding and Support

Some parents with food-allergic kids also admit to feeling isolated from families that do not have to worry about food allergies. Many of them say that parents of kids without allergies simply cannot comprehend the pressure they are under every day. "After my son was rushed to the doctor because he touched an egg noodle—just touched it—my friends finally apologized to me for what they'd been saying about me behind my back,"[51] says Kathy Franklin, a mother in New York City. Another parent, Heather, has a young daughter, Hailey, who is severely allergic to egg and dairy products. "I cannot list an aspect of our life that has not been affected by the diagnosis," she says. "When people caution me at parks that while Hailey climbs well for a young child, we need to be careful, I laugh and reply facetiously, 'You don't know the half of it. She's safer next to a pit bull than a glass of milk or a scrambled egg.' They just don't get it, and unfortunately, too many people don't."[52]

Fortunately for Heather and other parents in her situation, many support groups for parents of children with severe allergies have been established in recent years. Some of these groups are community-based. Others are lodged on websites that allow parents all across the country—and around the world—to talk to one another about food allergy issues. These sites can be an invaluable resource for information on food allergy symptoms and treatments, menu planning tips, recipes, and strategies for navigating allergy challenges at home, day care, school, camp, and college.

As part of an awareness program, the Food Allergy and Anaphylaxis Network publishes a series of children's books about food allergies.

In addition to providing information on managing specific food allergy issues, websites maintained by groups like Allergy and Asthma Network Mothers of Asthmatics enable parents to talk to each other about the emotional challenges of caring for children with food allergies. Many moms and dads treasure these connections with other parents who "know what it's like." As one parent of a child with severe allergies to peanuts and eggs writes, "I needed to share our joys and sorrows along the path of life. My friends who didn't have a food allergic child couldn't understand my consternation over preschool and kindergarten. When I shared this with other parents of food allergic children, they understood exactly my fears."[53]

Support networks also exist for children, teens, and adults who are themselves dealing with severe food allergies. Most of the major organizations engaged in food allergy research, education, and advocacy maintain online forums to help people with food allergies find support and encouragement. Many teen-friendly books have also been published on this subject. These works acknowledge that food allergies can be "particularly frustrating in your teenage years, when thoughts of dating and college overshadow the importance of remembering to read food labels," writes physician Paul M. Ehrlich. "Becoming a teenager no doubt comes with increasing independence, but it is important to remember that with independence comes great responsibility, especially if you are a teen with a food allergy."[54]

A Part of Who You Are

The daily lives of individuals with severe food allergies—and their families—are full of challenges. They have to be on guard at all times against accidental exposure to potentially deadly allergens. Some activities and foods that most people take for granted are either off-limits for them, or have to be undertaken with extreme caution. As a result of all these factors, people with food allergies sometimes experience embarrassment about their condition. These feelings typically reach a peak during their teen years, when many youth feel intense pressure to conform to their peers and look and act like everyone else.

Despite all of these hurdles, though, millions of children, teens, and adults with food allergies lead rewarding and interesting lives. They play sports, travel to exotic lands, pursue artistic or musical passions, and go to dances and parties like everyone else. They often eat well, too. As Wood writes, "clearing the cupboards of the foods that ail you doesn't condemn you to a lifetime of rice cakes and distilled water. The world offers an abundance of tasty and nutritional substitutes for the most common troublesome foods, and the food industry is pumping out more variations each year."[55]

Finally, some people whose lives have been changed by food allergies

FOOD FACT

According to the National Institute for Allergy and Infectious Diseases, people with egg allergies should avoid taking vaccines for influenza, yellow fever, or rabies.

insist that they have found their medical condition to actually be a benefit. They say that it has taught them to better appreciate the simple things in life. Some families and friends also say the challenge of managing food allergies has strengthened their emotional bonds to one another. Others indicate that they and their loved ones developed some of their finest personal qualities thanks to their food allergies. "Living with food allergies has made [my son Peter] the person he is today," says his mother, Leslie. "And if you ask him, he wouldn't have it any other way." Leslie acknowledges that raising a child with severe food allergies can be exhausting and nerve-wracking. She also insists, though, that her son's food allergies have shaped his family's life in a variety of beneficial ways. "You will realize who your real friends are, and better yet, your child will realize who his/her friends really are at a very young age. Your child will value life, and will have compassion for people with differences."[56]

Introduction: Navigating the World of Food Allergies

1. Sandra Beasley. *Don't Kill the Birthday Girl: Tales from an Allergic Life.* New York: Crown, 2011, p. 4.

Chapter 1: Explaining Food Allergies

2. Claudia Kalb. "Fear and Allergies in the Lunchroom." *Newsweek,* October 27, 2007. www.thedailybeast.com /newsweek/2007/10/27/fear-and -allergies-in-the-lunchroom.html.
3. "Food Allergies." KidsHealth.org, October 2008. www.kidshealth .org/kid/ill_injure/sick/food_aller gies.html#.
4. Robert A. Wood, with Joe Kraynak. *Food Allergies for Dummies.* Indianapolis: Wiley, 2007, p. 12.
5. Laura Beil. "Little by Little: As Food Allergies Proliferate, New Strategies May Help Patients Ingest Their Way to Tolerance." *Science News,* September 12, 2009, p. 20.
6. Susan Dominus. "The Allergy Prison." *New York Times Magazine,* June 10, 2001. www.nytimes .com/2001/06/10/magazine/the -allergy-prison.html?pagewanted =all&src=pm.
7. Dominus. "The Allergy Prison."
8. Dominus. "The Allergy Prison."
9. Kevin T. Higgins. "Allergens and Labeling: Got It Under Control?" *Food Engineering,* March 2006, p. 58.
10. Elizabeth Landau. "Allergy Injectors are Liberating and Daunting." *CNN Online,* September 4, 2009. articles .cnn.com/2009-09-04/health/food .allergies.bees.epipen_1_injector -allergy-patients-allergic-reaction ?_s=PM:HEALTH.
11. Wood. *Food Allergies for Dummies,* p. 53.
12. Dominus. "The Allergy Prison."

Chapter 2: Understanding Rising Rates of Food Allergies

13. Rebecca Fadel King. "A Plea For My Daughter." *Newsweek,* June 9, 2008, p. 21.
14. Kalb. "Fear and Allergies in the Lunchroom."

15. Katie Moisse. "Food Allergies in Kids: More Common than We Thought?" *ABCNews.com,* June 20, 2011. http://abcnews.go.com /Health/AllergiesFood/food -allergies-kids-common-thought /story?id=13866478#.TuYzSFb 7P85.

16. Quoted in Dominus. "The Allergy Prison."

17. Beil. "Little by Little," p. 20.

18. Elisa Meyer. *Feeding Your Allergic Child: Happy Food for Healthy Kids.* New York: St. Martin's, 1997, pp. 9–10.

19. Quoted in Mike Stobbe. "Food Allergies Up Among US Children." *Associated Press,* October 23, 2008. http://articles.boston.com/2008 -10-23/news/29272312_1_food -allergies-amy-branum-milk-and -egg-allergies.

20. "Allergy Attack: More and More Americans Are Getting Allergies. Why?" *Weekly Reader (WR) News, Senior Edition,* May 7, 2010, p. 4.

21. Kalb. "Fear and Allergies in the Lunchroom."

22. Quoted in Dominus. "The Allergy Prison."

24. William E. Walsh. *Food Allergies: The Complete Guide to Understanding and Relieving Your Food Allergies.* New York: John Wiley, 2000, p. 15.

25. "Food Allergies." KidsHealth.org.

26. Quoted in William E. Walsh. *Food Allergies.*

27. Walsh. *Food Allergies,* p. 260.

28. National Institute of Allergy and Infectious Diseases. *Guidelines for the Diagnosis and Management of Food Allergy in the United States: Summary for Patients, Families, and Caregivers.* Washington, DC: U.S. Department of Health and Human Services, National Institutes of Health, 2010, p. 12. www .niaid.nih.gov/topics/foodAllergy /clinical/Documents/FAguidelines Patient.pdf

29. Meyer. *Feeding Your Allergic Child,* p. 10.

30. Melinda Beck. "New Rules for Food Allergies." *Wall Street Journal,* December 7, 2010. online.wsj.com /article/SB10001424052748704 15630457600338289487345 2 .html.

Chapter 3: Diagnosing Food Allergies

23. Quoted in Tara Parker-Pope. "Telling Food Allergies from False Alarms." *New York Times,* February 2, 2009. www.nytimes. com/2009/02/03/health/03well. html.

Chapter 4: Scientists, Lawmakers, and Food Makers Respond

31. Tess O'Brien-Heinzen. "A Complex Recipe: Food Allergies and the Law." *Wisconsin Lawyer,* May 2010. www.wisbar.org/am/template .cfm?section=wisconsin_lawyer

&template=/cm/contentdisplay .cfm&contentid=92733.

32. O'Brien-Heinzen. "A Complex Recipe."

33. Quoted in Food Allergy and Anaphylaxis Network. "Food Allergy and Anaphylaxis Management Act Becomes Law." FAAN, January 5, 2011. www.foodallergy.org/page /food-allergy-and-anaphylaxis -management-act-becomes-law.

34. Beil. "Little by Little," p. 20.

35. Wood. *Food Allergies for Dummies,* p. 162.

36. Kalb. "Fear and Allergies in the Lunchroom."

37. Higgins. "Allergens and Labeling: Got It Under Control?," p. 58.

38. Higgins. "Allergens and Labeling: Got It Under Control?," p. 58.

Chapter 5: Adjusting to Life

39. Wood. *Food Allergies for Dummies,* p. 243.

40. Quoted in Mary Brophy Marcus. "Food Allergy Sufferers Find Socializing Tricky." *USA Today,* January 7, 2010. www.usatoday.com/news /health/2010-01-07-allergies07 _CV_N.htm.

41. Annie Jorgensen. "A Message from Miss Wisconsin's Outstanding Teen 2011." Food Allergies in the Real World. www.faanteen.org/personal stories/miss_outstanding_teen _message.php.

42. "Telling My Teammates About My Food Allergies." Food Allergies in the Real World Web site. http://www .faanteen.org/school/teammates .php

43. "Bullying." Food Allergies in the Real World.

44. "Growing Up with Food Allergies." Food Allergy and Anaphylaxis Network. www.foodallergy.org /page/growing-up-with-food -allergies.

45. Brophy Marcus. "Food Allergy Sufferers Find Socializing Tricky."

46. "Food Allergies." KidsHealth.org.

47. Pete Wells. "Beating Eggs." *New York Times Magazine,* March 8, 2009, p. 43.

48. "A Successful Night Out." Food Allergies in the Real World. www .faanteen.org/personalstories/night _out.php.

49. "A Whole Lotta Love." Food Allergies in the Real World. www.faan teen.org/personalstories/lotta _love.php.

50. Wood. *Food Allergies for Dummies,* p. 244.

51. Quoted in Dominus. "The Allergy Prison."

52. "The Night Our Lives Changed." FAAN: Food Allergy and Anaphylaxis Network. www.foodal lergy.org/page/the-night-our-lives -changed.

53. Nicole Smith and Robert Smith. "Our Story of Food Allergies and Allergic Reactions." AllergicChild .com. www.allergicchild.com/our _story.htm.

54. Paul M. Ehrlich, with Elizabeth Shimer Bowers. *Living with Allergies.* New York: Facts On File, 2009, p. 102.

55. Wood. *Food Allergies for Dummies,* p. 287.

56. "How Food Allergies Can Shape the Person You Become." FAAN: Food Allergy and Anaphylaxis Network. www.foodallergy.org/page /how-food-allergies-can-shape-the -person-you-become.

allergen: Something that causes an allergic reaction.

allergy: A disorder of the immune system that causes the body to treat harmless substances as threats.

anaphylaxis: A severe allergic reaction that affects the whole body; symptoms can include terrible abdominal pain, difficulty breathing and swallowing, skin rash, and nausea and vomiting.

antigen: A chemical or other substance that produces an immune response upon being introduced into the body.

antihistamines: Drugs that combat allergic reactions by suppressing the impact of histamines.

cytokine: A chemical released by the immune system.

diagnosis: Identifying a disease or ailment based on medical tests and symptoms.

epinephrine: A hormone that opens the breathing passages and increases heart function.

epinephrine autoinjector: A syringe-like medical device that delivers epinephrine to people suffering from allergic reactions.

heredity: The passing of traits from parents to offspring.

histamines: A chemical released by the immune system that triggers many allergy symptoms.

hygiene hypothesis: Theory that improved cleanliness and effectiveness in fighting germs is increasing our vulnerability to food allergies.

protein: A natural substance found in meat, fish, eggs, and other foods that helps our bodies develop and remain healthy.

American Academy of Allergy Asthma and Immunology (AAAAI)

555 East Wells St., Ste. 1100
Milwaukee, WI 53202-3823
Phone: (800) 822-2762 or (414) 272-6071
Website: www.aaaai.org

The AAAAI website contains special sections for patients/consumers with a wide range of useful information, including a searchable directory of allergists. The site also includes a Just for Kids section with puzzles, games, and videos pertaining to food allergy issues.

Asthma and Allergy Foundation of America (AAFA)

1233 20th St. NW, Ste. 402
Washington, DC 20036
Phone: (800) 727-8462
Website: www.aafa.org

The AAFA touts itself as the oldest organization for people with asthma and allergies in the world. It provides educational information and community-based services to people in the United States through regional chapters and support groups. The group also funds research into allergy treatment and cures.

Children's Digestive Health and Nutrition Foundation (CDHNF)

1501 Bethlehem Pike
P.O. Box 6
Flourtown, PA 19031
Phone: (215) 233-0808
Website: www.cdhnf.org/

CDHNF is a valuable resource for medical professionals and patients interested in learning more about food allergies, as well as celiac disease and other digestive disorders.

Food Allergy and Anaphylaxis Network (FAAN)

11781 Lee Jackson Hwy., Ste. 160
Fairfax, VA 22033-3309
Phone: (800) 929-4040
Website: www.foodallergy.org

FAAN is a multifaceted advocacy organization that plays a leading role in educating Americans about food allergies and anaphylaxis. The site details the group's many education, advocacy, and research efforts, and it also links to FAAN's teen-centric website, called Food Allergies in the Real World.

Food Allergy Initiative (FAI)

1414 Avenue of the Americas, Ste. 1804
New York, NY 10019
Phone: (212) 207-1974
Website: www.faiusa.org

Founded and maintained by the parents and grandparents of children with food allergies, FAI funds food allergy research, sponsors educational programs on allergies, and lobbies the federal government on food allergy policy.

Kids with Food Allergies Foundation

73 Old Dublin Pike, Ste. 10, No. 163
Doylestown, PA 18901
Phone: (215) 230-5394
Website: www.kidswithfoodallergies.org

The foundation provides educational information on all facets of coping with food allergies. It includes one thousand food recipes searchable by allergens that commonly need to be avoided.

FOR MORE INFORMATION

Books and Articles

A. Anderson. *Flourishing with Food Allergies: Social, Emotional, and Practical Guidance for Families with Young Children.* Southbury, CT: Papoose, 2008. This book combines stories from parents with advice from medical professionals to provide a guidebook for navigating the various everyday obstacles that food allergies present. It includes tips for safe eating at birthday parties, schools, camps, and friends' homes.

Sandra Beasley. *Don't Kill the Birthday Girl: Tales from an Allergic Life.* New York: Crown, 2011. A sensitive, funny, and informative memoir that provides lots of insights for children with allergies and their parents and other caregivers.

Linda Marienhoff Coss. *What's to Eat?: The Milk-Free, Egg-Free, Nut-Free Food Allergy Cookbook.* Lake Forest, CA: Plumtree, 2000. This popular and highly regarded recipe book contains instructions for making more than 145 meals and desserts that are free of dairy, egg, and nut allergens.

Susan Dominus. "The Allergy Prison." *New York Times Magazine,* June 10, 2001. This long article tells stories of how severe food allergies can influence every aspect of life for allergy sufferers and their families.

International Food Information Council Foundation. "Understanding Food Allergy," 2007. www.foodinsight.org /Content/6/FINAL_Understanding -Food-Allergy_5-22-07.pdf. This informative brochure provides a summary of important food allergy issues, including diagnosis and treatment information for families of allergic individuals.

National Institute of Allergy and Infectious Diseases. *Guidelines for the Diagnosis and Management of Food Allergy in the United States: Summary for Patients, Families, and Caregivers.* Washington, DC: U.S. Department of Health and Human Services, National Institutes of Health, 2010. www.niaid .nih.gov/topics/foodAllergy/clinical /Documents/FAguidelinesPatient .pdf. A valuable resource for families with food allergy issues, this booklet provides recommendations on how to diagnose and manage food allergies. It also provides a starting point for patient-doctor conversations about food allergy precautions and treatments.

88 Food Allergies

Scott H. Sicherer. *Understanding and Managing Your Child's Food Allergies.* Baltimore: Johns Hopkins University Press, 2006. An informative, practical, and sensitive book that guides parents, teachers, school nurses, and other caregivers through all aspects of caring for a child with food allergies.

Robert A. Wood, with Joe Kraynak. *Food Allergies for Dummies.* Indianapolis: Wiley, 2007. Written and arranged in a user-friendly manner, this book covers all aspects of food allergies, including many tips on living safely and happily with allergies.

Michael C. Young. *The Peanut Allergy Answer Book.* Minneapolis: Fair Winds, 2006. This book is an informative and authoritative reference tool for families, teachers, and other caregivers affected by peanut allergies.

Websites

Allergic Girl Resources (www.allergic girl.com). This website offers coaching, consulting, and advocacy services to empower people with food allergies. Founded by Sloane Miller, the author of the critically acclaimed book *Allergic Girl: Adventures in Living Well with Food Allergies,* the website also includes several entertaining and informative blogs related to food allergies.

Allergies Health Center (www.webmd .com/allergies/default.htm). This section of the popular WebMD website offers a wide range of information on food allergy issues.

Food Allergies (kidshealth.org/kid /ill_injure/sick/food_allergies .html#). This section of the popular KidsHealth.org website provides a kid-friendly explanation of how food allergies work. It also includes tips on how people with food allergies should adjust their diets.

Food Allergies in the Real World (www.faanteen.org/index.php). This website maintained by the Food Allergy and Anaphylaxis Network (FAAN) is designed specifically to help teenagers with food allergies. It includes advice and information on all sorts of teen social issues that are complicated by food allergies, from dating to dealing with bullies.

Food Allergy Kitchen (www.food allergykitchen.com). This site provides practical cooking and eating solutions for people with food allergies or sensitivities.

Information about Food Allergens (www.fda.gov/Food/ResourcesFor You/Consumers/SelectedHealth Topics/ucm119075.htm). This website maintained by the Food and Drug Administration (FDA) provides basic background information on food allergies to consumers and includes links to other governmental sources.

G

Genetics, 36–38
Gluten, 21

H

Histamines, 14–15
Hygiene hypothesis, 34–36
Hypochondria, 30

I

IgE (immunoglobulin E), 13–14, 46
Immune system, 12, 13–14
    hygiene hypothesis and, 34–36
Immunoglobulin E (IgE), 13–14, 46
Insect bites, 12

J

*Journal of Allergy and Clinical
    Immunology,* 29
Journal of Pediatrics, 51

L

Lactose, 15
Land v. Baptist Medical Center (1999),
    55–56
Legislation
    federal, 53–56, 58
    state, 59

M

Mast cells, 14
Meals, allergen free
    learning to cook, 71–73
    when eating out, 73–74, 75
Medical histories, 45
Milk, products containing, 22

N

National Institute of Allergy and
    Infectious Diseases (NIAID), 45, 47,
    79
National Institutes of Health (NIH), 29
NIAID (National Institute of Allergy
    and Infectious Diseases), 45, 47, 79
NIH (National Institutes of Health),
    29
Nursing, link between food allergies
    and, 38

O

Obama, Barack, 58
Oral food challenges, 49
    double blind, *41*
    types of, 50–51

P

Parents, clashes with children over food
    rules, 74–76
Peanuts/tree nuts, *24*
    increase in allergy rates for, 29
    products containing, 23
    school bans on, 57, 58

R

Rash, *13*
Rehabilitation Act (1973), 53–55
Research, on cure for allergies, 59–62

S

School Nutrition Association, 58
Schools
    accommodation of children with
        disabilities in, 54–56, 58
    banning of peanuts in, 57, 58

PICTURE CREDITS

Kevin Hillstrom is an independent scholar who has written extensively on health and environmental issues. His works include *U.S. Health Policy and Politics: A Documentary History* (2011).